ALWAYS IN MY BLOOD

ROBERT NG

DEDICATION

I dedicate this book to my wife Jade and all my family and friends.

CONTENTS

Preface

This story is related through the eyes of a Liverpool lad born in 1945 to mixed parentage. It reminisces through his journey of life from early childhood days through the innocence of youth, into adulthood. Thrust from the comforts of a happy family home into the Merchant Navy and onto an adventurous roller coaster ride, encompassing highs and lows and the inevitable relationships along the way.

It takes the reader to far flung exotic ports, in South America, India, Hong Kong, Japan, Australia, South Africa, Pacific Islands and to the distant shores

Robert Ng

of New Zealand, stirring memories with a cocktail of emotions, fun filled, happy, exciting, sometimes difficult and very often painful.

Every individual has their own personal views on life and situations and the writer is relating to how events felt to him as a young man. This is a reflection of times based on his early life and time spent in the Merchant Navy.

In cases where the author has been unable to contact and gain permission to use real names, he has changed those names and identity features for the purpose of privacy and confidentiality. Due to the passing of time and capacity of memory, parts of the story are fictionalised to keep the flow. It has also not been possible to relate word for word what was actually spoken. This, hopefully, does not detract from the content of the narrative

Prologue

I was tired bruised and dirty; blood was running down my chin, the taste of fresh blood filled my mouth and I was half sitting half lying on the floor.

Seconds before, after being questioned about who I was I had answered truthfully that I was, only in overnight and the suit I was wearing was mine. Next a shout of "LIAR!" followed quickly by a blow to the mouth, knocking me cleanly off the chair. The unexpected fall to the floor didn't give me time to react. A sickening crunch was felt to the back of my head as it hit the wooden panelling on the wall, the effect of which seemed to reverberate through my whole body. Dazed and shocked I looked up at the large overweight ginger haired official standing over me. His fists were clenched and his face was getting redder by the second. He then again accused me of pinching a warder's suit to try to escape.

I prepared to defend myself from the next onslaught.

How had I got into this mess? It seems so long ago now.

Always in My Blood

Chapter One - Early Days

Growing up

I was born in 83 Cambridge Street in Wavertree Liverpool on 30th November 1945 to mixed parentage. My mother was Mary Elizabeth Jones, from Liverpool born of a Welsh father and English mother. My father Hung Ng originated in Guangzhou (formerly known as Canton) in the Guangdong Province of Southern China.

May and Hung on their wedding day

Mum and dad decided that in the event of children, dad would name the boys and mum the girls. Dad gave the lads Chinese names and mum credited the girls with English names. As a consequence I was named Tensing and my younger brother Garsing. Later on in life, I changed my name to Robert, mainly to help in my career as a sales manager. It was hard enough having to explain my surname spelt Ng and pronounced in many different ways. As a family, we used the pronunciation Ning.

I look back now and marvel how things have changed since I was a child. We had an old tin bath hung on a nail on the whitewashed backyard wall. The outside toilet was cold, damp and draughty; torn squares of newspaper pushed onto a nail served as toilet paper. Smells seemed to linger; no such things as deodorant sprays in those days. Not a place to spend time, especially in cold weather. It was in and out as fast as possible. Bath time was once a week and the rest of the week it was vest off and a good rubdown with cold water and carbolic soap, but if grandma happened to be about, she would treat us to her favourite soap, which was Fairy toilet soap. For toothpaste, we used baking powder or salt.

At bath time, mum boiled a kettle of water on the coal fire and we had to take turns using the same bath water, occasionally topped up with new hot water from the kettle. I remember mum testing how hot the water was with her elbow. Many a squabble over who got to use the first bath ensued, usually the girls got to use the bath first, I think that being a boy it was determined, boys tended to get a little grubbier than the gentler sex. You can imagine the state of the water! Mum or grandma would then scrub the quarry tiles in the kitchen and the residue was used to swill down the yard.

There were no such things as washing machines, we had a dolly tub, scrubbing board, mangle and washing line, or for drying indoors a wooden clothes maiden. We thought we were really posh when dad installed a pulley rack in the kitchen, which was operated by using the pulley to take it up to the ceiling and out of the way. As the family grew, mum and Davina had to take the main wash to the local corporation washhouse. I sometimes waited outside to help them carry the washing home. Mum would say to me "*You can't come in here! Men aren't allowed*". As a six year old, that sentence really aged me, but in the back of my childlike thoughts, I was quite proud to be called a man.

On a hot day I would play marbles in the gutter with other boys. One of the older lads had a supply of ball bearings, he seemed to take delight in smashing his opponents brightly coloured glass marbles. In the end nobody would play with him until he went back to normal glass marbles. The girls would play hopscotch, a children's game, drawn on the pavement, where children would hop in and out of squares to retrieve a marker thrown into the squares. Sometimes we would play tick with a ball of compacted newspaper. We were delighted when one lad produced a rubber ball; it became a much faster paced game.

I remember wooden spinning tops; brightly coloured with chalk marks or coloured metallic paper that you sent spinning with a small leather whip. One of my favourite toys was called a Circus Top. It was made of tin and brightly decorated with circus scenes. You had to pump it up and down to set it spinning. I was also the proud owner of a set of lead soldiers; my favourite lead toy was the battleship *HMS Warspite*. When I lost it on the way home from school, I spent hours on my knees covering the route home. Mum sent a search party for me because I was so late. Even then as the evening darkened I was reluctant to give up my search. This of course was before lead was deemed dangerous. Yes, simple toys but they created hours of fun.

Circa 1952, outside our house in Huyton, Mum and dad with me, Davina Jennifer, Gar and Lynne

Mum would pop outside every half hour or so to check on us and to smoke a cigarette. I think mothers would take it in turn, so we were never left alone for long. I remember thinking all the mums look alike with their scarves tied up like turbans and a cigarette not far from their lips.

We would then struggle all the way home, with me insisting on a larger bundle of damp washing than my little frame could sensibly carry. After all, I was a man!

I was highly delighted when dad managed to salvage and repair an old black prestige carriage pram. Mum used it to ferry the washing between home and the washhouse. This meant rather than carry the washing home, I was able to ride with it.

I remember feeling the cold quite a lot and all the family sitting round the fire, often resulting in chilblains; a painful swelling irritation on hands or feet caused by poor circulation in the cold. I also remember having holes in my socks, but grandma would tell us to take them off so she could darn them at the first sign of wear. I remember grandma trying to teach me how to darn. Stupid I know but I used to make the small holes in my socks larger so I could try out my newfound skills. To get a brand new pair was a treat, but initially we were only allowed to use them for best; on Sundays, or going to Sunday school, which was a simple church service for children. I looked forward to going to Sunday school but not for the right reasons, mainly because we were given picture cards to collect. We would swap the doubles with other children, each of us endeavouring to have the first full set.

Another special occasion we enjoyed was visiting relatives. Mum or grandma would deck me out in white shirt, grey short pants, grey knee length socks and white pumps. There was always a ritual Sunday mornings, Grandma would whiten our pumps and boil the white shoelaces. On arrival we would be on our best behaviour. On many occasions people would remark to mum, "*what wonderful, well behaved children you have.*" Mum and grandma were very strict as to the way we behaved ourselves in other people's homes, so misbehaving was not an option. Although we had nothing, it was important to put on a respectable face to the rest of the world.

There were no such things as computer games then, or even computers! Our evenings would often entail playing board games such as Ludo or Snakes and Ladders. I loved a card game called Chase the Ace; everyone seemed to get animated and excited as we endeavoured to pass on the dreaded ace. Grandma used to favour Ludo, young and old would play together, real family entertainment. Television was still in its infancy and was for the very rich; in fact, none of our friends had one. I always remember grandma saying, "*It will never take off*".

Yes, leisure time in the evenings was very much a family affair. We would gather around the fireplace, mum or grandma would join in, as we played Ludo. Grandma used to hate losing she tended to get rather stroppy if anyone made her forfeit a counter. We all got wise to the situation we took to counting along with her, when it was time for her move. We discovered she could be prone to cheating to win the game! We were fascinated by some of the poetry that mum or grandma would recite. One such piece called "*Tommy Mouse*" was used as a bedtime story. Thanks go to brother Gar for remembering the words.

Tommy Mouse

Oh mother dear cried Tommy mouse, I've found a house to let
The door stands open, and inside the dinner's ready set
We're very crowded here you know, with such a lot of mice
So, don't you think we should remove? we'd do it in a trice.
Oh no! Oh no! Cried mother mouse, all shaking in a fright
if you should touch that dinner Tom, you would be in a plight
The open door would quickly shut with such a dreadful snap
And never more would I see you Tom, that house is called a
TRAP!

Another poem with endearing sentiments is one which grandma recited to us during our childhood.

Somebody's Mother

The woman was old and ragged and grey and bent with the chill of a winter's day
The street was wet with the fallen snow and the woman's feet were aged and slow
She stood at the crossing and waited long, alone, uncared for, amid the throng
Of human beings who passed her by, nor heeded the glance of her anxious eye
Down the street with laughter and shout, glad in the freedom of school let out
Came the boys like a flock of sheep, hailing the snow piled white and deep.
Past the woman so old and grey, hastened the children on their way
Nor offered a helping hand to her, so weak, so timid, afraid to stir,
Lest the carriage wheels or the horses' feet should crowd her down the slippery street
At last came one of the merry troupe; the gayest laddie of all the group
He paused beside her and whispered low, "I'll help you across, if you wish to go".
Her aged hand upon his strong young arm she placed, and so, without hurt or harm, he guided her trembling feet along, glad that his own were firm and strong
Then back again to his friends he went, his young heart happy and well content
She's somebody's mother, boys, you know for all she's aged and poor and slow
And I hope some fellow will lend a hand to help my mother, you understand
If ever she's poor and old and grey when her own dear boy is far away
And 'somebody's mother' bowed low her head; in her home that night, the prayer she said was, "God be kind to that noble boy, who's somebody's son, both pride and joy.

Mary Dow Brine (1816-1913)

Another poem we kids requested over and over again had a more sombre tone; it was just after the end of the war and the target was Adolf Hitler.

Hitler's Dream

Here is a story, strange it may seem, of Hitler the Nazi and his terrible dream;
Being tired of his allies, he lay down in his bed and amongst other things, he dreamt he was dead
He was all straightened out and lying in state, and his little moustache was frozen with hate
Then from this earth to heaven went straight, and proudly walked up to the golden gate
But, Peter looked out and in a voice loud and clear said, "Hitler the Nazi, you can't come in here!"
So Hitler turned back and away he did go, with the greatest of speed to the regions below
A lookout angel, well worth his hire, flew down to Satan and gave him the wire
Satan said "Fellows, I'll give you a warning, we're expecting Heir Hitler down here this morning,
But I'll tell you straight and I'll tell you clear, we're too blasted good for that fellow down here"
"Oh Satan, Oh Satan", Heir Hitler cried, I heard what you said while standing outside,
Give me a corner, for I've nowhere to go", but Satan said, "Nix! A thousand times NO!"
He kicked Hitler back and vanished in smoke, and just at that moment, Heir Hitler awoke,
He sat up in a lather of sweat, crying "doctor, oh doctor, it's my worst dream yet,
To heaven I won't go, that I can tell, but it's a damned awful thing to be kicked out of Hell"

The youngest in our family was my sister Barbara. We share the same birthday albeit a ten-year difference. Throughout the years, she has been able to compose poetry to fit any occasion. Barbara has a wonderful way with words; all with little twists of humour that people of all ages can understand and relate to. One of her poems, I think better describes the way things have changed, than I could ever put into words:

Barb's Poem

"Just sitting here thinking, of how things used to be many, many moons ago, or it seems like that to me!
When only those with money, possessed a telephone and ONLY Colour TVs, were found inside their home!
A car was such a luxury, the symbol of success and men were Lord and Master and women second best
when families played together, inside their homes and out No Internet to rule the world; no scary hooded lout!
The holidays were spent in campsites near and far and families of seven, were sandwiched in one car!
Messages took ages, for emails weren't around and 20 silver shillings amounted to a pound.
No Internet, no emails, flat screen TV and more No wonder Mum had seven kids! and I had less than four!"

One day, dad who worked in the restaurant business, brought a live chicken home. I took it to be a pet and treated it as such. I named her Beaky. She took up residence in our backyard. Beaky strutted and postured around as if she owned the place. I fed her and tried to train her and over a few days, I became very attached. One morning I rushed out to feed her, I said to dad, "*Beaky has escaped*!" only to find to my horror she was in the oven. I cried and cried and no amount of cajoling would persuade me to eat her. Feeling hungry, I had to make do with jam butties. It wasn't often we had the luxury of chicken. It took a few years before I could eat any without thinking of Beaky.

The coal man delivered coal on a horse and cart. After he had deposited ours into the coalbunker, gran would hand us an old sack and say: "*follow the coal man and pick up anything he drops*". We would follow him for a few streets and we got to know him quite well. It soon became apparent he would drop more than normal so we wouldn't have to carry the sack back too far. We'd rush home, hands and faces blackened from scooping the slack up (small bits of coal and coal dust). Grandma would scrub our hands with a small scrubbing brush, carbolic soap and cold water. I always remember my hands feeling quite sore afterwards. No such thing as a gentle scrubbing brush for my delicate childhood hands

I remember having holes in my shoes and having to stuff them with newspaper and cardboard to stop the damp and cold invading. In school, I would endeavour to keep my feet flat on the ground, to stop any cruel jibes about the state of my footwear. However if it rained it meant I spent the rest of the day uncomfortably squelching around until I got home. It was shoes off; dry them out by the fire and a refill of dry newspaper.

Looking back times must have been hard bringing up a growing and increasing family. My parents spent all their hard-earned money on the family, no luxuries for themselves.

Mum would borrow money from the Provident man. The Provident was a company that issued small loans in the form of Provident cheques that could be spent in specific shops. Mum would spend the money on shoes for the kids or whatever the family needed most and it was conveniently repayable over 52 weeks. Some weeks when money was particularly scarce mum would tell us to hide when the Provident man called for payment. Mum would then hope to be able to pay him the following week.

I remember one Christmas time when money was short; somebody gave dad an old rusty tin pedal car. He spent many hours of labour transforming it into an American tank made of

Jennifer and Lynne in dad's DIY Tank

plywood and painted dark green with a large white star emblazoned on the bonnet. In brown wrapping paper, it sat in pride of place next to the small Christmas tree. That frosty Christmas morning I was pedalling it up our road, fighting my way through slush and snow feeling on top of the world in my shiny new tank, the local kids had other thoughts, they pretended to be Germans and bombarded me with snowballs; they called them hand grenades.

I didn't take it out much after that, because when the snow thawed, their chosen missiles became stones and rocks; playing-out was quite tough for a seven year old. We had nothing, but we had a loving caring family and that was everything. Washing machines, dishwashers, television, central heating, hot and cold water on tap, computers and the digital age; the world has changed so much in my short lifetime. One wonders what the future holds as the rate of innovation speeds up year on year.

June1953 we celebrated the Queen's Coronation with street parties. The photograph below shows dad with the Crown Jewels cake that he made and decorated. Upon the base stood a very elaborate Crown with an authentic looking red velvet cap. The jewelled crown was made with royal icing, silver balls and coloured icing 'jewels'.

Dad with the Coronation Cake in Seacroft Close Street Party

Supernatural

One particular event will remain with me forever; it concerns

Rupert Bear Book

the paranormal. We lived in Seacroft Close in Huyton, which is a suburb of Liverpool and at that time I was seven years old, lying in bed reading a Rupert Book. The memory has become so ingrained on my mind I remember the cover; it showed Rupert with a hoop and a stick. Auntie Clara gave me this book along with a box of tin toys, from her childhood. After some research I was lucky enough to find a copy of the book on the Internet.

17

It was mum's 31st birthday and celebrations were in full flow downstairs. The small house was filled with friends and relatives. The music blaring from the record player "*Do not forsake me oh my darling*", by Frankie Lane, one of dad's favourite singers, made it difficult to sleep.

As tiredness washed over me, I took off my glasses and put them on the floor under the iron bedstead. I threw the book on the floor and at the same time grabbed the blankets to pull over my head and turned my body towards the window. Out of the corner of my eye, I saw a blurred shape hovering above the window ledge. Without my glasses I squinted to focus, my heart skipped a few beats as into view emerged a little old man. He was very wizened with wrinkled features, silently laughing and his belly jiggling. His body seemed to rise out of the window ledge. It was a body without legs!

Terrified and shocked, with my little heart thumping, I dived under the blankets, screaming for help. It seemed ages, but was possibly only seconds, maybe minutes but nobody came. I lifted the blankets to find the blur right alongside the bed, back to the sanctuary of the covers once more, expecting invisible hands to rip away the blankets, exposing me to this ghostly apparition. I scrambled across the bed to the opposite side, nearest the door shouting and screaming as I went, one foot out of the bed. He reappeared floating in front of me blocking my escape route; just then the door burst open. Dad, mum and other partygoers crowded into the small bedroom. My father grabbed me and mum shouted, "*What's the matter? What's the matter?*" I ran sobbing from the room and straight downstairs, refusing to go back. The party guests crowded around me trying to comfort me. The general assumption was that I had had a nightmare. Mum told me not to be silly and that I had been dreaming.

For many weeks, I would not go into that room alone. I didn't like to even venture up the stairs. However, time is a great healer, it wasn't long before I started to believe the nightmare explanation.

Some years later the wizened old man reappears, we'll come to that later....

Newcastle upon Tyne

Dad went into partnership and opened The Maykway Chinese Restaurant Northumberland St, Newcastle upon Tyne. Detrimentally it meant him being away from home for weeks at a time. Working long hours with only one day off a week, he had to save up his days off to travel back to Liverpool, which enabled him to spend a few days with his family.

After many months it all became too much for him and the family so a decision was made to apply for a transfer/exchange to a council house in the north of England.

Mum and dad moved the family to 29 Binswood Avenue, in Newcastle upon Tyne, which was a newly built house in an area called Blakelaw on the fringe of the city. As a child of eight or nine years old, the Geordie accent to me was like learning a new language. I struggled to understand what was going on and no doubt my Scouse accent didn't help. Expressions like "away man come here" threw my childhood brain into disarray. The other children were equally flummoxed by my attempts at communication.

The property was a lovely three bedroomed semi-detached house with a small front and large back garden. Dad spent every spare minute sieving the back garden to the depth of 3 feet to provide a good foundation for his latest hobby of growing fruit, vegetables and beautiful flowers.

England was still in midst of rationing, so providing food for the family was a great way to add that little extra to the dinner table. Dad was also very generous to our close neighbours and friends always picking a little extra for them. As children we raided the garden on many occasions, eating the garden peas, which were my favourite, leaving empty pods as evidence of our pilfering. After one foray mum caught us red handed and shooed off the garden. Later Dad asked us to collect some peas for Sunday lunch, but we could only gather enough to barely cover the bottom of the saucepan. He sat us down and spoke at length about taking things, and said we only needed to ask. As usual the lecture did the trick, I never touched the peas again. We ended up having to suffer sprouts, which I disliked with a passion.

Once a week the mobile shop would appear, Gran would send us out with our ration books to get whatever was needed or allowed. I remember one disastrous day when I received the biggest smacking on the back of my legs ever. The back of the van was full of queuing neighbours, my friend and I were confronted by a display of boiled sweets, in our boredom we pretended to grab a sweet, without even touching them. We then pretended to pop it in our mouth and say "yumm"! It was just the excitement of seeing sweets! I suppose we were very baby-like in our actions. However the shopkeeper angrily reprimanded us and asked us to open wide, seeing no sweets in our mouths he accused us of swallowing them. Unbelievably they were what were known as Gobstoppers, it would have taken a child 20 minutes to eat one. The shopkeeper then sent for mum who smacked my legs till they were red raw all the way home! She said *"don't you ever show me up in front of the neighbours again no child of mine is going to grow up as a thief."* I felt really hard done to, and really hurt that mum thought her little lad was a thief, no amount of explaining would persuade her to believe otherwise. A stupid childish prank caused me to be in the black books for weeks.

I remember spending two particularly bad winters in Newcastle upon Tyne. I believe 1953 and 1954 were two of the worst winters on record, not only for the amount of snow, but also the horrendous fog and smog, which was caused by the thousands of house and factory chimneys churning out coal burning smoke. It was so dense you could barely see three feet in front of you; the visibility was so poor. Because of it's yellowish tinge a smoggy day became known as a "*pea-*

souper". During those winters, thousands of people died across the country. Later on legislation was put in place to control the coal burning emissions.

We had lived in Newcastle for about 18 months, but after a disagreement in the business partnership, dad decided to take up an offer to work as a chef in Manchester. My cousin Eric was about 19 years old, when he and his girlfriend Nancy came up for a weeklong holiday. They arrived in a Majestic Siddeley, which belonged to Eric's father; uncle Albert. Because the family was in the throes of moving back to Liverpool, Eric agreed to let my brother Gar and me travel back with them in the car.

We felt rather posh being chauffeured from Newcastle upon Tyne back to Liverpool. We were heading back to Liverpool the city of our birth that mum missed so much.

Mum, dad, Davina, Lynne and Jenny were to follow a few days later by train. The youngest Sandi was still a babe in arms, being born in Newcastle and the only Geordie in the family. Sandi in later years went to great trouble to mathematically calculate where she was conceived, to prove she was a scouser like the rest of us.

Anyway, here we were, travelling in style in an Armstrong Siddeley, a car that was usually seen carrying Royalty and Police officials. The backseat squeaked a little as I wriggled to find a relaxing position on the highly polished pleated black leather seats. The interior gleamed with chrome and polished hardwood trim. It was a poor mans Rolls Royce explained Eric. Although we felt far from poor, as we trundled from town to town, watching the local populace staring as we passed. Bear in mind, private cars in the early fifties were few and far between.

The very majestic 'Armstrong Siddeley', similar to Uncle Albert's

There were four of us travelling in the car Eric and his lovely girlfriend Nancy, and brother Gar and myself. Things were going well and it was a really lovely drive; an adventure to two young boys. Unfortunately just before Catterick the engine clattered and thumped its way to a violent end. Eric managed to manoeuvre his way to the grass verge, lifted the bonnet then thrust his head in his hands as he realised the extent of the damage. On his arrival, the garage mechanic confirmed that the big end had broken apart and ploughed into the sump.

Although I was only nine at the time I felt so sorry for Eric. This was his dad's pride and joy, and I could see in Eric's eyes he was anxiously agonising on how he was going to break the news to his Dad. They towed the car back to the garage. Eric, Gar and I were sitting in the open back of the pickup truck and Nancy sat up front with the Mechanic. As we were only halfway through our journey, the garage owner kindly offered to drive us into Catterick, which was the nearest town, where we were able to catch a bus into Liverpool. The bus unfortunately was very full as many soldiers were going on leave, so we all had to stand up for most of the way. What a comedown. It certainly brought us back to earth with a bang. "The highs and lows of travel in the 50's."

On a few occasions throughout this book that I've mentioned co-incidences but none are so amazing as this next one.

My sister Sandi was talking to her next-door neighbours Leslie and Linda Armstrong, discussing the repairs needed for the fence that separated their back gardens. Although they had lived in the house for three years, Sandi had never met them. They were telling her that they had lived in France for some years but sold up and came back to Liverpool. They were a friendly and chatty couple and Sandi soon learned that Leslie was a year or so older than her and had spent his youth in Speke where our family had grown up and that he had attended the same school as the children in our family. Linda added that Leslie is a Geordie. Happy to meet a fellow Geordie, Sandi told them, "oh so am I!" She went on to tell them that she was born in Newcastle upon Tyne in a place called Blakelaw. Leslie said, oh, I lived in Blakelaw too, in Binswood Avenue. This was a surprising revelation, as Sandi knew that this was the road that we moved into. She said, "I lived in number 29", but Leslie said he couldn't remember the number but would ask his older sister, Olive who had a very clear memory of their time in Newcastle. From what we knew though it was unclear if we had lived in the road at the same time.

A few days later Sandi saw Linda again who told her that no, we couldn't have lived in the road at the same time because the too had lived in number 29 Binswood Avenue.

Later on that week Sandi spotted Linda and Leslie working in their back garden, she called through the fence to say hello. After a few minutes of chat, Leslie asked, "did you live in Withington Road"? "Yes", Sandi replied, quite surprised. She went on to tell them that we moved from Newcastle when she was a young baby into number 28 Withington Road. Leslie delivered a shock when he told Sandi that his sister Olive had told him that they had lived in number 28 Withington Road and our parents had exchanged houses.

Leslie's mother missed Liverpool very much and a few years later, they moved back to Speke. Leslie and his siblings attended the same school as my siblings and me.

It seems an amazing co-incidence that Sandi and Leslie should live next door to each other 60 years after living in the same house, which was 177 miles away.

It's okay... it's okay!

After moving to Speke it wasn't long before my little sister and the youngest of our family Barbara was born on my 10th birthday.

For dad, travelling to his job in Manchester from Speke was hard work on top of a 14-hour day, particularly in the mid 50's, there were no motorways then, and it was quite a struggle especially in adverse weather.

One weekend dad asked me to accompany him, as he was short staffed. I was probably 12 years old at the time, and along with the other siblings often helped out in places dad worked. This time he needed a dishwasher for a very busy weekend.

At the time, dad owned a Renault 750; a small car that was a cross between the Morris Minor and Volkswagen Beetle but uglier. It had what were commonly known as suicide doors! They were hinged in the middle so that the opened the opposite way around. However it was dad's first car and he was very proud of it.

The morning was bitterly cold, and we spent ten minutes scraping ice off the windows. I don't believe the car had a heater, so we were well wrapped up in pullovers, scarves and coats and gran's hand knitted gloves.

A Renault 750, similar to dad's - note the suicide door

The weather conditions were horrendous: the road was like an ice rink. We slid and slithered onto Central Way, and although it was a main road it was just as hairy as the side roads. The inside front windows eventually cleared with lashings of de-mister liquid. It was 6.30 in the morning and I was struggling to stay awake, tiredness took over and I fell into a deep sleep.

The sound of screeching tyres and grinding metal jolted me back to life. I awoke to a vision of the yellow de-mister bottle sailing past my head. What was happening? I could only watch as the sky replaced the ground a number of times in succession in what seemed to be in slow motion. I looked across at dad. He was grimly holding on to the steering wheel saying *"It's okay... it's okay!"* At the same time my body was like a bag of rags as I was flung around the car; no seat belts back in those days!

My head and shoulders engaged with the roof a couple of times then we lurched to a sudden stop with the nose of the car pointing skywards. I frantically fought to open the door. As it opened backwards I had a great difficulty but eventually managed to scramble over it. Then I found myself sailing about 5 feet into an ice-covered ditch. My feet crunched through the ice and freezing water entered my shoes. I scrambled up the ditch to find dad on the other side of the car. He shouted, "*You okay?" "Yes, are you? "Where are we?"* I replied. Dad explained that we were on Widnes Road just before Penketh. I was violently shaking mainly with shock, but the bitter cold didn't help. Dad put his arm over my shoulder and held me tight, "*Thank god we are ok*," he said. We stared at the car in silence.

The back end of the car was down in the ditch, the front sat atop a gorse bush that formed a hedge along the road. It looked a real mess, the roofline over the rear seats had been badly squashed; it was just as well we didn't have back seat passengers. Steam was rising from the engine in the rear of the car and the engine was still running, but any attempt of climbing up and retrieving the keys was ludicrous.

Another car travelling in the opposite direction stopped. A woman carefully made her way across the road. We were expecting an offer of help, even just a lift to somewhere a little warmer. The first words we heard were uttered in an American accent "*Can I take a photograph*!" Before dad had time to answer she promptly took one, turned and said "*Thanks*" jumped in her car and was off! I couldn't believe it. She didn't even ask if we were okay.

The next vehicle that came along was a van; the driver pulled up and enquired if we needed help. He drove us to a pub about half a mile away. The pub named *The Cuerdley Cross* will always be engrained on my mind. Because of the early hour we had to knock and wake the landlord. He kindly let us in and proceeded to light a fire.

It's amazing to think how times have changed. He offered and gave dad a double Brandy to calm his nerves! No such thing as Breathalyzer tests in the 50s. He telephoned the police, and was informed that the police would be there in half an hour.

A policeman arrived in a black Ford Zephyr. He said *"show us where your car is then,"* On the way he kept commenting about drivers can't handle a bit of bad weather, I was really annoyed as his barbed comments seemed to be aimed at dad. Just before the bend in the road where our car had skidded, the policeman lost control of his car and we ended up facing the way we had come. The red faced policeman had to admit the conditions were far worse than he thought.

I found great pleasure that the obnoxious policeman was embarrassed by his own driving skills.

Bullies

We lived in a small three bedroomed council house in Speke, which was an overspill estate in the south of the city. Dad, being very artistic, dexterous and practical was forever putting his own stamp on it. I recall a hand built wooden fireplace that from a short distance looked like it was made from beautiful Italian marble and one day the front room ceiling was painted to resemble the sky with white fluffy clouds. For the little money we had, it was dad's way of adding a bit of luxury to our lives.

If any of us stepped out of line, dad had a wonderful way of putting us all back on the right track. He would sit us down and identify our wrongdoing with a parable. He never smacked us, but sometimes we felt so bad afterwards I think we all would have preferred a good smacking.

If we misbehaved when dad was away, mum was not averse to smacking our legs, but it didn't do us any harm. Worse than that, she would threaten us with, "*Wait till your dad gets home*". I would do my best to make amends rather than face the dreaded parable. On reflection, we have a lot to thank our parents for. They taught us respect, humility, the art of loving life and caring for those around us. To this day, I can honestly say that there has never been a cross word between us and we keep in touch on a regular basis, due I believe to our upbringing from two wonderful parents.

Our little house, by today's standards, was somewhat overcrowded. There were five girls and grandma sharing one bedroom; mum and dad were in another. The small front bedroom was allocated to my brother Gar and me.

In the early days, being of mixed race was something out of the norm. We never embraced the Chinese culture and rarely, if ever, mixed with Chinese people as we were brought up away from Liverpool's Chinatown. All the family were very English in outlook and so felt hurt by the racist bullying that went on at school. Many a skirmish in the playground followed racist taunts. Wearing National Health glasses didn't help. Kids can be quite cruel; "*chinky four-eyes*" was just one of the milder names that I recall.

I was always a skinny kid and not particularly good looking so I found the bullying quite hard to take. My father insisted I must stand up for myself, not be intimidated. "*Easier said than done*", I thought, as four or five lads often carried out the intimidation. I found that if I took no notice; gave them no ammunition, the sniping toned down, although the class bully would endeavour to stir things up again. My father's advice was to stand up to him.

This was settled near the school bike sheds, where a fistfight took place. I seemed to be getting on top when one of his friends hit me on my back with a cricket bat. I went down on my knees, totally winded and in considerable pain. Another of his heroes then kicked me in the stomach. Thankfully, the mathematics teacher intervened and he frog-marched us off to the headmaster. "*So you like fighting do you lads?*" asked the headmaster. "*I am arranging a supervised boxing match for you both in the gym*". So badly bruised was I that he arranged it for two week's time.

I was really angry with the bat-wielding thug that I asked if he could arrange a match with him also. The head arranged that for one week later.

The ensuing weeks were peppered with threats as to what fate was going to befall me. I must admit it all felt very daunting, but dad's words echoed in my ears, "*Act calm, show no fear and the adrenalin will carry you through; only by meeting this head on will you be able to hold your head high, win or lose".* Dad showed me some defensive moves and blocks. These moves related to karate and I told him *"This is a boxing match, it won't be allowed".* He said, *"These moves will strengthen your stance and you will not be knocked over easily, most of all you will present yourself as a much tougher opponent".* He added, *"Do not panic, defend well and pick your moment to strike".*

On his day off he would spend time with me, teaching me how to strengthen my position and take command of the ring. He taught me how to block and counter-attack, *"The most important thing is to remain calm and not panic yourself into mistakes"* he said. He then went on to explain, *"Being calm always unsettles bullies, as they expect the opposite reaction from their victims".* After a few lessons I was almost looking forward to the confrontation.

The days passed quickly and the fight neared, my confidence grew and sure enough the adrenalin kicked in and I was rearing to go. I fought the class bully for five three-minute rounds. Tactically, my opponent surprised me. He came out of the corner arms flailing as if in a panic to get the fight over as quickly as possible. He seemed to have no plan, but to bulldoze his way through the fight, relying on his extra weight.

Dad's words focused my thoughts. I stood my ground, defended his wild punches, taking a few hits, but the more he hit me, the more strength I found to fight back with better judged punches.

Being a much bigger lad than me, by the third round his bulk and wild fighting style started to take its toll, slowing him down. He became cumbersome and easier to hit. He didn't like it; I was starting to embarrass him in front of his friends. Every time a decent punch caught him out he would whine to the games teacher who acted as referee. The final bell rang and the referee declared a draw. Not a bad result, as I had visions of it lasting one round with me on my backside. The fight had earned me respect from the rest of the class. The bullying stopped from then on.

As for our friend the cricketer, he pulled out of the fight and was full of apologies.

I soon came to realise, the more I stood up for myself and fought back, encountering many a bloody nose, knocks and scrapes on the way, the easier it became. Like all bullies, they went on to target less difficult prey.

Corporal punishment

I awoke with a shock; the large wooden blackboard duster bounced off my desk and glanced the side of my face as it went flying across the classroom. *"Ng!! Describe a semiquaver... Not listening are you Ng, didn't you get any sleep last night? Stand outside... and report to Mr Kneale's office after assembly in the morning"!*

I stood up glancing down at the indentation in my desk, and thinking... *"Shit! That could have been my head*!" Music lessons bored me silly; Mr Lythgoe's monotonous droning voice negated all of my efforts as I struggled to keep my eyes open.

The night before, my brother Gar and I had sat on the stairs and listened surreptitiously to the radio; a programme called 'Quatermass' was on. We had managed to follow the series often just through a small crack in the door. Grandma said it was too scary for kids to follow. Crazy I know, but I think she still thought of us as little boys. However, Grandma was unaware of our presence as we strained to hear every word from the living room. The slightest movement from the front room sent us scurrying back up the stairs suppressing laughter.

I stood outside the classroom door, glancing through the small glass panel; Mr Lythgoe's outburst certainly caught the attention of the class as they listened intently to his every word. My mind could not escape thoughts of Mr Kneale's brutal cane and six of the best from the headmaster the next morning. He seemed to take pleasure in inflicting as much pain as possible and if you so much as flinched, the next stroke was applied with even greater gusto. It wasn't the best way to start the day.

I was 14 years old coming up to 15 and looking forward to the end of term, as I would be leaving school to make my way into the big wide world of work. Like most lads of that age I was still undecided what to do. I loved drawing and art but financial restraints prevented me from following my chosen course. I had dreams of being a sign writer, or cartoonist. However coming from a large family I needed to work and help pay for my keep.

I had often worked in restaurants during summer holidays and had gained some catering experience and contacts: a possibility.

Mum and dad worked in the Meccano factory, Binns Road in Liverpool. Meccano was famous for making Dinky Toys (model cars) Hornby Train Sets and Meccano Sets. Mum had told me she had spoken to the foreman and that a job was available as a labourer if I wanted it. It didn't sound particularly exciting to me. Dad worked 12-hour shifts with only a half hour for lunch and no tea breaks. If you needed to use the toilet you had to put up your hand to be excused for five minutes. To top all that he often came home with nasty burns from the molten metal that spat from the die cast injection machine. Many years later I was fortunate to meet Mike Egan, who had worked alongside dad in the next Kip (booth). He told me that dad was the top bonus earner because he worked so hard and a lot of the burns he had was because of the fearless ways he worked. Mike was a lot younger than dad and related a story, which often made him chuckle. He informed dad that he would like to learn to speak the Chinese language. Dad's reply in broken English, "*You can't even speak English*!" It was comforting to hear that he thought a lot of dad and had a great working relationship.

Mum's job, along with a long line of women, was spraying the little cars; not as precarious as my dad's but heads poised over the spray booth every day must have caused health issues. We were later informed that the paint used had a high lead content.

I kept glancing up at the school clock; time seemed to stand still as the big finger edged its way to 4 o'clock. The bell lethargically jangled above my head. To me it was a starting bell. I was off and had a head start as I raced down the corridor. From behind, Mr Cliff's voice boomed after me, "*Stop running lad*!!" I slowed down to a canter and picked up the pace once again as I emerged from the confines of the building.

I ran down Stapleton Avenue and headed home, in a hurry to take our faithful German Shepard dog Trixie for a walk. Since a pup we had a special affinity and I loved taking her for long walks. All the family adored her so it was first home that had the privilege of her company. As I ran up the path the excited yelps of Trixie greeted me through the glass panelled door. I fought to open the door as Trixie jumped up and down, inadvertently pushing it closed from the inside. Trixie was a big dog and a little on the heavy side, mainly due to being spoilt and overfed by the Ng household. I ran upstairs and changed from my school clothes, grabbed a jam butty (sandwich) and sought out Trixie's lead. We left the house just as the other siblings were arriving home, It was my favourite time of the day as I headed to Oglet Shore with Trixie straining and panting on the choker, aware that in minutes she would be roaming free, retrieving a small tennis ball on the hills and cliffs of Speke shoreline.

Mum, dad, Gar and myself dressed for Christmas at the 'Great Wall' Restaurant in Southport

Out for the count

Dad was often away working as a chef and we would look forward to him coming home, always with a small present for each of us. Mum and grandma worked hard looking after our large family unit, five sisters and a brother. Money was tight; we would often have to borrow half a loaf of bread, until the next day from our more affluent neighbours. On occasions the lights would go out. We scrabbled about looking for old foreign coins that fitted the electric meter to keep the lights on during the darkening evenings. Mum looked forward to the meter man calling, as we always received a rebate, but with the foreign coins put on our pile, it was never as much as anticipated, however mum would put them in a tin ready for the next emergency.

Davina the eldest sister had, from an early age, helped run the household. She was a little dynamo always finding work to do, lessening the burden for mum and gran. I must admit, I was a bit of a practical joker and looking back sometimes a torment and pain in the backside to our hardworking eldest sister Davina.

On one memorable occasion Davina was up to her eyes in work using what can only be described as an industrial sized rolling pin, rolling out a pie top. I stepped over the washing basket in our very cramped kitchen to squeeze past Davina. As I passed, I mischievously pinched the skin on the back of her arm. Bad move. I woke up about 5 minutes later wondering what had hit me. The back of my head sported an industrial sized lump. Davina, in reaction, had just hit out with what she was holding. I made a mental note not to do that again. Another time I was teasing her as she was opening a tin of dog food for our Alsatian dog, Trixie. She flung the tin at me. I ducked and it went sailing through our sitting room window, smashing the pane. The upshot of that encounter was grandma gave me a good smacking for ducking!

The summer holidays are another time I remember well. We all had to work to help with family finances. Dad was the chef in The Great Wall Chinese Restaurant on Lord Street, Southport. Most of us spent our holidays working, either in the kitchen, the tearoom, or waiting on in the restaurant. As a waiter, I became quite adept at carrying and balancing plates of food and soup.

One particularly hectic lunch-time during the Easter period I was carrying five bowls of tomato soup downstairs from the kitchen; three in my right hand and two in my left hand. I lost my footing at the top of the stairs to bump down from stair to stair on my backside, juggling the bowls of soup all the way down. As I reached the bottom, in my momentum I stood up and carried on walking without spilling a drop! Queuing customers on the lower staircase burst into applause.

I often think what a great YouTube video that would have made had we had the technology!

With such a large family, it must have been very difficult to make ends meet. Dad and mum worked tirelessly to pay the bills, but one thing we had in abundance was an outstanding family unit, full of warmth and love. I can only remember hard but happy times.

My education results were never bad and I always managed to keep in the A stream with results slightly above average, going through school only to secondary education level. I

1964 – Outside our house in Speke – from left: Lynne, Davina, Gar, Jenny, Mum, Dad, my friend Bob, family friend Richard. In the front: Barbara and Sandra with our Alsatian Trixie. In the background is a pram with my newly born nephew David. I was home on shore leave and behind the camera!

excelled at Art, Woodwork and Metalwork. I loved creating things with my hands; I suppose it was something in the genes inherited from dad. The important subjects like English and Mathematics were just above average. Average in our school should have read adequate, as I don't believe the standards were that great.

Owing to family financial circumstances, education was not a priority, getting out and earning a wage to supplement the family income had to be top of the agenda.

Chapter Two – Leaving Home

Call of the sea

Wayne Yeates was the seaman, who was responsible for igniting my desire to go to sea,

I met him while walking our Alsatian dog Trixie, just after my fourteenth birthday. Wayne was almost seventeen at the time. As I was passing, he remarked on the size of Trixie. We got talking and the conversation turned to the Merchant Navy and his career at sea. We kept in touch and became great friends. On leave, he would mesmerise me with tales of exotic far-flung ports around the world. He always looked a million dollars, suntanned, new suit, well groomed, taxis everywhere, with no end of girls showing an interest in him. I thought, "*This is the life for me*"

Wayne told me in later years that the time he met me, he had only been going away to sea for two to three months and the farthest he had been was France on a coaster. His early tales were just elaboration! Still, they were elaborate enough to set me on course for approximately 9 years in the Merchant Navy.

I made enquiries at the age of fifteen and pestered the Shipping Office, known as "*the Pool*" on a weekly basis. I was fortunate as they took me on without the training that was usually required. I believe this was because I had helped in restaurants that dad worked in as a chef. As I was going into the catering department as galley boy, I had all the qualifications needed! This was great news because a six-week course at the Nautical Catering College opposite Mann Island in Liverpool would have been the alternative. Six weeks would have seemed like six years in those heady exciting days after my acceptance.

My first ship was MV Crinan, which was a Denholmes ship carrying iron ore between Algeria and the UK. She was a new ship but ore dust disguised the clean lines that she later presented. The princely sum of £16 a month was my pay, supplemented with a little overtime. I sent £8 a month home for the family. My first impression was that the ship was very industrial, after all, it was an ore carrier and although dirty and grimy on the outside, once inside I could see that the ship sparkled.

I signed on as a catering boy and was responsible for scrubbing the officers' alleyways on my hands and knees before breakfast.

MV Crinan

My duties also included cleaning senior officers' cabins, in fact anything to do with the catering or housekeeping side. The ship also employed a galley boy and his work involved mainly kitchen and store duties. Whilst in port, scrubbing was an everyday occurrence, as the iron ore dust filtered its way onto every surface. After three days, what seemed like a never-ending rerun of scrubbing and polishing the same surfaces, I began to wonder what had I let myself in for? I also wondered why lads have to endure a six-week course to learn how to clean. The first days dulled my expectations of the glamorous life on the ocean wave. On leaving port the never-ending ore dust subsided, as the ship was completely hosed down and the exterior gleamed as brightly as the inside accommodation.

It was crazy I know but, three days out of Liverpool and proceeding to Bone in Algeria, I was already feeling homesick. Besides a few days at Colomendy School Camp this was the first time I had been away from the family.

The ship was rocking around a bit after entering the Bay of Biscay and the radio officer predicted a strong deterioration in the weather. An attempt at playing darts in the mess room was curtailed, as it became difficult to even stand up, so hitting the dartboard had become an art in itself. A dominoes session started up and some of the lads had thrown wet tea towels on the mess room table to stop the dominoes sliding about. I joined in for a half hour or so, then retired to my cabin to read.

In the early hours of the morning somebody fumbling under my bedclothes groping and touching my privates rudely awakened me. In total darkness I grabbed the hand and blindly struck out. My fist connected with some soft tissue, which I found later to be his throat. I shouted out, he answered back uttering, "*Shhh Shhh Shhh*". I cursed at him and dived for the light switch, taking in a disgusting smell of stale beer and smoke, knocking him off his feet as I passed. The light revealed a drunken middle-aged greaser still pleading with me to be quiet. I was trying to push him out of my cabin. My door burst open and from the alleyway three passing sailors, alerted by the commotion, dragged him out and gave him a beating there and then. They then dragged him to the bridge, to face the Captain. The rest of the crew treated him with contempt. It must have been a relief for him to arrive at Bone in Algeria where he was relieved of his duties and paid off for gross misconduct. It was a shocking thing to happen to a lad three days into a seagoing career. Throughout the trip, I kept my cabin door locked.

Algeria had just gained independence from France. On arrival, we found the port to be a hive of activity. The French Army was pulling out and the port was in turmoil, as squadrons of army personnel loaded waiting naval ships with all manner of supplies. Everybody seemed to be in a rush and in the chaos, before our very eyes a forklift truck loaded with mattresses skidded off the end of the quay and into the harbour, driver, mattresses and all. About twenty quick thinking soldiers dived in to rescue the mattresses. I suspect their enthusiasm to do this was an excuse to escape the blazing midday sun. It seemed that there was a lot of bad feeling against the French, so the local populace were helping them on their way.

Posted on the gangway was a notice WARNING: SHORE LEAVE AT YOUR OWN RISK underneath read YOU COULD BE VIOLENTLY ATTACKED IF MISTAKEN FOR FRENCH NATIONALITY. What a blow, my first time abroad, after days of looking forward to experiencing a completely new culture, our hopes seemed dashed. After lunch, following much hesitation and indecision, one of the deck lads and I decided to risk a short jaunt ashore. We nervously made our way into the dusty sand filled town. Near the centre of town, we found a *souk* (market place). From all directions, the vendors set upon us.

"Come to my shop everything free",
"Very high quality leather",
"Best Souvenirs in Algeria",
"Free refreshments in my cousin's shop",
"American! American! This way, very cheap",

I was worn down by one vendor and reluctantly bought a leather stuffed camel about 10 inches tall but looked beautifully made. We haggled as is the custom, but according to the big grin on his face he got the much better deal. After half an hour, we decided we had had enough, so made our way to a quieter part of town.

Half a dozen children, playing football, some in bare feet started following asking for cigarillos. I didn't smoke so my friend was the target of their requests. He naively opened a packet and offered one to a young lad who suddenly snatched the whole packet and took off in the direction of the souk, with my friend on his heels. The lad ran straight to a group of youths shouting "*Frenchy! Frenchy*"

That's when we took off pursued by about eight youths hurling abuse and rocks. We ran as fast as we could before realising we were on the wrong side of town and moving further away from the docks. The mob grew larger as other youths joined them; the streets were also getting quieter. They split up, trying to outflank us. In desperation we tried to skirt around the edge of town. We thankfully stumbled upon a busy street. We then ran into a large souvenir shop bought a load of rubbish with the proviso that the shop owner would get us back to the ship. He went outside to speak to the youths milling around the entrance. To this day, I don't know what he said but they slowly dispersed.

He explained, in broken English that it was not safe for us to attempt to make our own way back to the ship, he then offered his services and said for a small fee he would drive us back to the ship. We spent the next half hour bartering. At one point, he even asked that we give up our watches as part payment. This we of course refused, he had to be content with what little money we had between us. Guiding and shoving us through the back of the shop, he then took us through a maze of shops and people's homes, avoiding the main streets, to a battered rusty sand encrusted pickup, lying in the shade of a dusty olive grove. We scrambled into the back and he covered us with dirty sacks and straw. In the midday heat, we lay there sweating and bouncing around on the gravel strewn steel floor, until he screeched to a halt outside the dock gates. He had provided two very relieved young lads passage back to the safety of their vessel.

As the years have passed, I often wonder if he had dramatized the situation we were in, to extract as much as possible from two very vulnerable and naive young lads.

That was my sole excursion ashore, on my very first trip to sea. If this was a taste of things to come, I was beginning to have second thoughts about my chosen career.

As for the stuffed camel, it started to fall apart after a week revealing blood soaked dirty bandages as stuffing. I threw it over the after end and watched as the wake of the ship churned it over, sending it to the bottom of the Bay of Biscay.

The camel, bought as a present, would have probably ended up on our mantelpiece. I don't think Mum would have been enamoured to find, blood soaked bandages protruding from its backside!

Seasick

If I recall correctly, the MV Pearl was my second trip away to sea. She was a small coaster belonging to Gem Lines. Dad drove me to Llanddulas to join her in his brand new Renault Dauphine car. Approaching Llanddulas via the top road, we saw a very small coaster rising just off the pier. Dad said, "*I hope it's not that one, it's so small. It may be very dangerous in heavy seas carrying stone*". However, scanning the horizon it was obvious this was the ship. Besides, no ship larger could gain access to the small wooden jetty.

We found that a local limestone quarry supplied the small coasters with quarried stone via a transhipment conveyor belt that passed under the main Abergele Road down to what looked like a rickety old wooden pier.

It was a very blustery day and the *MV Pearl*, already loaded had pulled away from the pier awaiting my arrival. As I clambered along the gravel and stone-littered pier,

MV Pearl

the ship moved in, bobbing up and down in the heavy swell, It was unable to berth due to the sea conditions. I had to time and then hurl my suitcase to a couple of waiting deckhands. I waited for the ship to rise within reach, hesitating a few times as she pitched wildly away at the last moment. I then jumped across the gap to the slippery wet deck. As I landed, the deckhands missed me and I slid and stumbled badly gashing my leg on the corner of the steel hatch. In those days, there was no such thing as 'Health and Safety'. With a grimace, I waved my father off. He had a look of concern on his face. I shouted, "*I'm fine*", rubbing my badly gashed knee.

Before introductions, I was helped into the accommodation and one of the engineers cleaned the wound and promptly stitched up my knee with 4 stitches before applying iodine. The iodine hurt more than the stitches.

The captain, a large hearty looking bearded Scotsman, introduced himself. The first words he said were, "*We are all taking bets; we've had four new lads over the last six weeks and they only last until the next port. These small coasters sort the men from the boys; I guarantee you'll be as sick as a dog until we reach Glasgow*". Being new to the sea and my first ship being a comparatively larger and more stable vessel, I had yet to experience seasickness. I was shown to my cabin and allocated the top bunk, the bottom occupied by one of the deckhands. I was surprised to find the top bunk had two leather straps. I enquired what they were for. "*You'll need them, otherwise you will be pitched out of your bunk in heavy weather. For safety's sake always strap one up when you go to sleep, in case the weather declines*", the young deckhand replied.

The *MV Pearl* was a very small coaster with a gross tonnage of only 1093. Her length was 212' 2" by 34' 1" wide with a 14' 7" draught. As we headed further into the Irish Sea the skies darkened and the weather did get a lot worse. Nausea silently crept over me and started to play havoc with my body. This I hid from other crewmembers, taking secret trips to the loo or the after end to rid myself of the retching that was taking over my whole being.

I felt so bad that I was finding it hard to concentrate on work. The smell of eggs and bacon sent me rushing off to the nearest refuge, at the same time trying to appear nonchalant and avoiding other crewmembers; I was too proud to admit that seasickness was taking its toll. Each time I encountered the captain he retorted "*Ar ye no sick yet laddie*?" "*No, I feel great captain*", I lied. Coming from a famous seagoing city, Liverpool, I wasn't going to admit the weather was getting to me. In truth I had not felt so bad in all my life, I felt dreadful all the way to the Clyde.

As on all small coasters, my job title "*Catering Boy*" really meant "*General Dogsbody*", I was responsible for not only catering matters but also all the cleaning and scrubbing of alleyways and serving in the mess. Captains Tiger (a term used for Captains Steward) was another of my duties. With a crew of seven it was all hands to the deck, we didn't even have a designated cook, so you can imagine the variety and type of meal that was dished up. One of the deckhands of some months standing had gained a reputation, as "*The worst cook on the seven seas*", as each time it was his turn, three or more of the crew would go down with a bad stomach. The job was eventually taken from him and he was made to clean the toilets instead. That was great news for me because that was one of my jobs. One boozed-filled evening he admitted doctoring the food because he hated cooking. He then became the target for whoever was cooking at the time. He left the company in Glasgow. The Captain then addressed the crew "*In a ship of this size everyone has to work together; we all need to be as fit as possible for any hazards that come our way. I will not tolerate any more antics like that*"

The weather had cleared as we entered the Clyde. Fluffy white clouds made way for the sun to bounce off the hills and dance across the waters. Such a lovely day to sit out on deck and bask in the warmth of the late morning sunshine, watching members of the crew casting mackerel lines overboard, fishing for our next meal.

The captain had two lines in his charge and was not having a lot of luck. He passed them to me to look after while he went for a mug of tea. What happened next was unbelievable. We must have run into a shoal, for as soon as he left, both my lines started tugging. With eight hooks on each line, it took me all my time to keep up. In fifteen minutes, I had landed forty-two large mackerel, far too much to consume fresh and so we had to salt two boxes for later. In two hours, the captain had landed only three fish. He couldn't believe it when he saw my tally. Being in the right place at the right time springs to mind. He took over the lines again and the result was; no more fish. It was so uncanny.

Over beautiful fresh mackerel that late afternoon, I was the talk of the table. The captain retorted, "*We can't afford to let you go now laddie, it's a good job you don't suffer from seasickness*" he exclaimed with a wink - and I thought I had him fooled!

Leaving Glasgow we navigated the Clyde and headed north, our next stop Norway with the cargo of limestone. Just north of the Shetlands the weather really turned violent. Thirty-five to forty feet waves hit the bow, each time the ship seemed to dive underwater, I feared for my life, then she would rise again, casting the seas aside. One minute I'd be looking straight up at the angry storm filled clouds, then as the ship crested the top of the wave, we would suddenly roller coast down again in what seemed a certain plunge to the bottom of the sea. The captain ordered all crew to wear life jackets at all times. A change of tactics was required. He would have to ride into the weather, thus making no headway. This was to prevent our stone laden ship from capsizing. I was on constant call, struggling up to the bridge, carrying large mugs of tea and sandwiches, no time for sit down meals, as all the crew were confined to stations. The view from the bridge was even more hair-raising. I recall thinking; "*I wish I was in a cinema watching this, not in a real life situation*".

For the next twenty-six hours, we were in limbo, not going anywhere. It must rate as the worst weather I have encountered in my entire seagoing career, I have never been so afraid; this includes typhoons and heavy weather in the Southern Ocean.

She was such a small vessel; we were thrown around like a cork. With rapidly diminishing fuel, even experienced seamen were praying for the weather to calm. Eventually, the Captain decided to try to head to the coast of Norway, to seek shelter in the nearest fiord. He informed the bosun it was a chance he had to take, otherwise with loss of power we would have turned turtle and the stone would have shifted taking us all to an early grave.

We made for shelter and the ship rocked and groaned under the strain. It sometimes felt as if the rivets would start popping. As the waves pummelled the ship, I suddenly realised I no longer felt seasick; fear and anxiety had taken its place.

Black thunderous skies and endless drizzle pursued us all the way to Odda in Norway. On entering the fiord, there was a feeling of relief as the weather cleared to reveal the most picturesque views. Brightly painted houses in the valleys lit up the landscape, waterfalls seemed to cascade everywhere. Everything looked so perfect, as if painted by an artist. It was such a peaceful and tranquil place after the violent and dangerous North Sea. The ship silently ploughed her way into port. I think we all breathed a sigh of relief as our feet touched dry land again.

The captain addressed me later that evening, "*That was a real test for you laddie, you'll never be seasick again*". True to his word that was the last time I ever felt seasick, but it was a tough lesson to learn.

Smuggling

As a galley boy, the low pay I earned and the money I sent home made it very difficult to enjoy what the world was offering. It soon became clear that if I were to make the most of all these exotic ports I was visiting, I would need another income source. Cigarettes on board were seven shillings and six pence for 200. As I didn't smoke I used to buy my rations and save them up to barter in upcoming ports of call. Senior Service or Capstan cigarettes were the easiest to sell. Woodbines never commanded as much money. Low pay served me well; because I needed the money, I never did have the temptation to smoke.

Wayne had advised me to buy some Yardley's Perfume from Woolworth. For a very small outlay, I made a profit of 300%. Carbolic soap was also a great earner. In fact, any British soap commanded good money in the early 60's. My pay was never touched as profits and wheeler dealing paid for my jaunts ashore and any presents I cared to buy. On some trips my locker would be full of all different products to trade, I remember: Pears Soap, Lux, Lifebuoy, Fairy toilet soap, Mum Rollette Deodorant, Nivea Creme and Old Spice aftershave lotion.

The Brazilian coast was my favourite, Rio de Janeiro in particular. The first line of sales was the customs officer who boarded the ship, as many of those officers already had contacts ashore to move the goods. British cigarettes and toiletry goods were in great demand, so they were operating a very lucrative business, highly illegal on their part, I am sure, but corruption was rife and besides it suited both parties. The customs officers would walk ashore blatantly carrying huge bags of contraband, so it was obvious that all ranks were involved. I never witnessed any drugs being smuggled; just cigarettes, tobacco, whisky and toiletries. Going via those officers also saved me and other members of the crew having to smuggle items ashore, with all the risks that entailed. On regular trips the customs officers became almost like friends, many on first name terms. The galley became a first port of call for them, as we fed them well and kept them supplied with beer.

It was also very easy to come unstuck as one young first trip deck boy found. He spent two months wages on a short wave Grundig Radio, which he bought in Tenerife, a tax-free bunkering port. His intention was to sell it in Santos, Brazil, to make some money to go ashore. A customs officer approached some vulnerable members of the crew, asking if any one had radios, transistor radios or watches to sell. The lad showed him the radio to which they negotiated and agreed a price. The officer told the lad to take it to the dock gates at 4pm where the officer would pay him the money. This unfortunately was a scam. Once at the dock gates, the same officer, who then threatened him with jail for smuggling, seized the radio. Panic stricken, the young lad gave up the radio and came back to the ship almost suicidal. Such an unfortunate introduction to a seagoing career, but it was too late, if he had spoken to established members of the crew, they would have warned him of the dangers. A lesson learned, but the poor lad ended up working most of the trip for practically no return.

That same trip we had word from our customs friends in Rio that there had been a crackdown in Recife our next port of call, approximately two days away. Talk about panic stations, the bosun who had really stocked up and had a glut of cigarettes and tobacco, spent the next two evening's building a stanchion, an upright post forming a support in his cabin to conceal a large stash of tobacco related goods, belonging to himself and other crew members.

We berthed in Recife late morning and were immediately boarded by what was called a scavenger party. They toiled into early afternoon searching the accommodation, whilst another party searched the engine room, hatches and rope lockers. The bosun invited me and the ships carpenter into his cabin for a beer; but it was mainly to help hide his hastily erected stanchion. The sound of the search party approaching had beads of sweat running down his weather worn features. A Gestapo type figure filled the cabin entrance, he brusquely ordered us to stand outside, whilst two of his men attired in white shirts and dark blue overalls, did a thorough search. As they were about to leave, the bosun offered the officer in charge a beer. Not a good move; he took the beer with only a grunt in the way of appreciation and then leaned back against the stanchion using it as a means of support. The bosun almost choked on his beer. Fortunately it held firm, however as he moved on to the next cabin we noticed that his pristine blue uniform sported a thick white line from shoulder blades to waist. We quickly vacated and locked the cabin and fled to lose ourselves amongst the rest of the crew. We wondered when he would find out he had been promoted with an extra stripe. It seems the stanchion had acquired a final coat of paint that very morning.

Five days later the make believe stanchion was removed and the contents sold to customs in Montevideo, Uruguay.

Returning up the coast and homeward bound, we called in at Rio again. The friendly customs officer informed us that the rogue officer had been badly beaten up for jeopardising the relationship with friends of the other custom officers. They said they managed to get the radio back, but had given it to a charity hospital...

Out on deck that night pigs were seen to be flying over the harbour and somewhere in the distance the crackle of a short wave radio disturbed the silence...

Think first

The next incident happened while serving on board the Salinas - a ship belonging to Pacific Steam Navigation Company (PSNC). We were en route to Columbia and Peru via the Panama Canal. Our first port of call was Tenerife for bunkers. I took the opportunity to purchase, tax free, a 9ct gold, slim, gents Ingersoll watch. It was adorned with roman numerals, quite fashionable in the sixties and quite a saving on the same model I had admired in Liverpool. However it was quite a big spend in relation to my earnings but I thought a good watch would serve me many years and still look good. Unfortunately, I cherished that prized possession for only nine days.

Our next port of call was Kingston in Jamaica. We berthed early morning and by lunchtime the temperature was in the high eighties. The majority of the crew thought it was too hot to venture ashore and decided to leave it until the temperature cooled in the evening. However being inquisitive by nature, I was in the habit of wanting to explore as soon as the gangway hit the quayside, work permitting of course. The ship's chippie (carpenter) known as big George was of the same disposition and he decided to accompany me ashore. After lunch we both walked out of the dock gates and, with the sun seeming to burn the back of my neck and penetrate through my T-shirt, we casually made our way through the rough area around the docks.

The pavements were crowded with men and youths, sitting against the walls, drinking, talking, some playing cards, often looking up at us and intently staring as we passed. The tension was palpable. Big George, a large broad shouldered Liverpool man in his early thirties, whispered, "*I don't like it around here, walk a bit faster*". We quickened our pace trying to appear nonchalant to disguise our increasing unease. Three youths proceeded to block the pavement in front of us. As we moved out into the road, they stepped out with us.

The largest of the group said, "*Hey slow down man, I got some good shit to sell you!*" By shit I surmised he meant drugs. "No thanks", I said, "*not interested*". By now we were surrounded on all sides. All of a sudden, as if in slow motion, I watched a scruffy man jump up from his sitting position, seize my arm and wrench the watch from my wrist, breaking the metal band in the process. In a split second he was off and running; I reacted instinctively pushing my way through the crowd in pursuit. I chased him for about five hundred yards, almost catching him, and then he darted up a narrow alleyway. There was a wall straight ahead. I thought I've got him now. As he turned to face me, I grabbed his arm trying to wrestle my broken watch from him. We wrestled on the gravel strewn dusty floor exchanging blows.

Suddenly from the top of the wall legs appeared and four more of the gang jumped down completely blocking my escape. *"Oh shit"*, I thought, *"how am I going to get out of this?"* One of the gang forced me back into the wall jabbing a wicked looking Bowie knife at my stomach, demanding my wallet. I kicked out wildly trying to ward them off. From my peripheral vision, I spotted another nasty character waving a knife. He only looked about fourteen, but was quite tall and gangly. I realised I was in real trouble. Then steaming up the alleyway my mate, big George, roared in his most aggressive scouse vernacular, *"F—K Off ya cowardly bastards!"* What a hero - he waded in with no thought for his own safety, immediately planting one of the mob on his backside. The surprise attack threw them for a minute and I was able hit out and connect. Blood appeared on the side of his face, he started screaming obscenities at me, but I couldn't understand a word he was saying, as he reverted to the local lingo. In the ensuing fracas, I was slashed on my left arm. Big George was hit over the head with a bottle and had blood running down his neck from a head wound. Such a gentle giant on the ship, he was swearing like a trooper. Strangely, though we were fighting for our lives, I felt no fear. Adrenalin was rushing through my veins so it was fight or die!

While all this was going on the thief made off with the watch. Then, out of the blue, a little old lady screamed at them from the entrance of the alley way. I cannot recall what she said, but it did the trick, they all suddenly scattered, some clambering back up the wall, while another tried to push past us back up the alley. A well-planted foot from George helped him on his way and sent him sprawling to the ground; scrambling to his feet, he made good his escape.

We thanked the old lady profusely for her intervention. She said, *"These men bad people, no good for Jamaica, we are a friendly happy people"*. She tended to George with a clean towel, clearing up blood that was running down the back of his neck. I was growing concerned for George, his head wound was bleeding copiously and the fact he had blonde hair made it look even worse. I said, *"We must find a doctor to have your scalp attended to."* He would have none of it. *"I can always get that sorted on the ship. We need to find a police station and report them bastards"*, he said. The wound on my arm, although bleeding heavily, was superficial and probably just needed a couple stitches. Our saunter ashore was now totally ruined; a sickening feeling tinged the air. However it was just a watch, we were lucky we still had our lives! I silently cursed myself for putting my mate in danger. I should have thought first before I gave chase, but in the heat of the moment my hasty reaction was activated by anger and injustice.

We approached an armed soldier patrolling a building to ask directions, but he totally ignored us; he was probably guarding a government building and not allowed to converse. We were constantly aware that we might be under surveillance from gang members. I noticed a large black hair protruding beneath my signet ring. As I extracted it, I realised it was a small piece of eyebrow consisting of a clump of bloodied meat with hairs. That put a smile on our faces, at least the beating hadn't been completely one sided. George said, *"Every time he looks in the mirror that bastard will have a scar to remind him we fought back. Not that it will stop them robbing the next unsuspecting seaman or tourist"*. A souvenir shop owner provided us with a map and directed us to the local police station.

At the police station, we reported the incident. They kept us waiting for thirty minutes, although nobody seemed to be overrun with work. They were mainly chatting and shuffling paperwork. The desk sergeant beckoned us and casually took details, giving the impression we were wasting his time. The sergeant eventually produced a map of the area and asked us to point out where the incident took place.

With a dismissive, tired tone, the sergeant wearily said, "*You two are very lucky. If I were you I would go back to the ship and thank the Lord you are alive. There have been three fatalities relating to knife crime in that area over the last three months. The gangs work in teams, that alleyway was a trap, part of the gang lie in wait, then they relieve you of anything else you possess*". George was really angry and ranted; "*You lot seem so laid back here why don't you do something about it then?*" "*We are very busy,*" replied one of the officers at the other side of the room, flicking over the pages of a newspaper he was reading with an inane grin on his face. This angered George even more, "*you want to get off your arse and do what you get paid for!*" Trying to calm the situation the desk sergeant suggested we went to the hospital for treatment. Big George replied, "*just give us a couple of aspirins I have a banging headache*".

I was particularly concerned about his condition because it was a head wound. I insisted we found a medical facility but George totally dismissed the idea. We didn't want to chance losing our wallets on the way back so we hailed a taxi. Back on board the Chief Steward tried to patch us up, but thought it better we seek expert medical advice. My wound was not too bad. There was more concern about George; head wounds are susceptible to all kinds of problems. The ship's agent was contacted and he took us for treatment to a medical centre just outside the docks. George had twelve stitches in three jagged head wounds; I only needed three. Some of the Liverpool lads went ashore looking for the guy with the missing chunk of eyebrow. But it was a senseless idea, the outcome of which could have had tragic consequences. However whilst in port he must have laid low as none of the crew ever caught sight of him.

It was an horrendous introduction to Jamaica. I did go ashore again as we were in port for three days, but we went ashore with caution and never less than four at a time, taking considerable care not to display items of value.

This experience provided me with another important lesson in life. I decided in future, being foolhardy had to be tempered with caution and 'a think before you act' mentality. I was fortunate that I had a future to look forward to. Things could have been so tragically different only for the bravery of big George and the interference of that little old lady.

In general the people were very friendly and happy. We had some great nights in some of the bars; the locals really knew how to party, reggae music was new to me, I loved the sound. I was fascinated watching the locals dancing in complete harmony to the beat. So I left with mixed memories of my short stay in Kingston Jamaica.

Just one beer

I spent some time with Ellerman & Papayani a company that sailed out of Liverpool, mainly to the Mediterranean. These were short trips that never usually lasted longer than six to seven weeks. The ships were very old, rusty and neglected. Accommodation was barely adequate and it sometimes felt that everything was held together by lashings of white and grey paint. This was usually applied on the return journey to the United Kingdom. Head Office was situated in Liverpool so the superstructure on returning home gleamed thus shrouding the rust beneath.

The Grecian was one such ship built in 1949 but looked much older than her years. Although I sailed on other ships in the fleet the SS Grecian holds many memories for me.

One of the runs was to Famagusta, Pathos and Limassol for potatoes, then onto Beirut, Lattakia, Haifa and Tel Aviv for fruit. They were great trips and I really enjoyed my time with that company.

SS Grecian

The homeport being Liverpool attracted a mainly Liverpool and North Wales crew, combining that with local understanding and humour, it was a recipe for a happy ship.

In 1963 Cyprus was torn with internal war. Tension between the Greek and Turkish ethnicities slowly increased. This was not helped by the destabilising influence and antagonism between Greece and Turkey. The United Nations along with 7000 troops and air support descended on the island on the 27 March 1963 to help stabilise the country and keep warring factions apart.

As we entered Famagusta harbour the blue helmets of the UN peacekeeping force sparkled in the sunlight. The old city walls that embraced the harbour were also manned. Pulling alongside, I aimed my new Yashica-Mat camera at the turret on the wall. I quickly withdrew it as the soldier lifted his rifle and barked out, *"No photographs."* My photo was safely on the film.

John Usher the second steward from Wallasey was a very good friend of mine. Now John liked his drink and like most of us, had an eye for a pretty face, this was almost his

UN No Photo's sign in Cyprus

undoing. After lunch the galley was scrubbed down, a quick change and we were ready to venture ashore. The fact that the town was almost on a war footing added to the tension, just going ashore became an adventure.

It was a very hot clammy day, the road was very dusty and the heat was suffocating. John was the first to spot a giant bottle of Keo beer above the door of a local bar. He said, *"C'mon lets grab a beer."* *"Later"* I replied, not wanting to waste any time to explore the town in the two short hours we had.

John being John insisted, so I said, *"Ok, just one."* We entered a gloomy sparsely furnished bar, with just four barstools and a couple of weather-beaten, uncared for tables; the only light coming from a soft drinks fridge wedged between the bar and Juke box. The bar was empty and we had to knock and call before an elderly, grumpy featured man shuffled from the living quarters. He gave the impression we had disturbed his siesta. *"What you like boys?"* he slurred. We ordered a couple of local beers. The beer slid across the wet bar, closely followed by a bowl of nuts. They looked as if they'd seen better days so we gave them a miss.

Then out from the back strolled a very attractive young lady. At first we thought she was the owner's granddaughter, but she turned out to be his daughter.

John was mesmerised and in the excitement, before he'd taken a sip out of his first drink, he ordered another. I protested and declined a second. The Bosun and one of the deck boys walked in, the jukebox started up and the Beatles latest hit "*I wanna hold your hand*" added life to the surroundings. With an eye on my watch I knocked back my beer and said to John "*Are you coming*?" "*I'm a bit tied up now I think she likes me*", he whispered. "*In your dreams, her main job is to keep you here spending money*" I replied. I bade my farewells and the Bosun and the deck boy followed me into town. The only excitement in the town was the large contingent of military on the almost deserted streets. The tension was palpable; it felt as if something was afoot.

Suddenly the ground shuddered with a deep 'Thump'. Our attention was drawn to a pall of dark grey smoke that rose between buildings near the dock area. "*Shit! what the hell was that!*" shouted the Bosun. The sleepy town came to life as sirens blared. A UN Toyota truck raced past, slowing only for two soldiers to scramble onto the open back.

We raced the mile or so back towards the port, an ambulance overtook us sirens blaring, soldiers seemed to appear in droves. In the distance barriers were being erected across the road, manned by UN troops in berets and blue helmets. As we got closer the local police confronted us, intent on directing us away down a side street. We hung back with a crowd of residents, straining our eyes through the dust and rubble ahead. Then I spotted it, the shattered plastic remains of the giant Keo bottle. My immediate thought was John! My god was he still in there?

Before my mind could unscramble, a voice shouted in my ear "*What the hell has happened*?" Relief spread over me. It emerged that after we left, the lovely young lady was joined by her boyfriend. John deflated, finished his drink and followed us up town. Losing track of us he could not resist the next bar. After settling down, he had heard the explosion. He finished his drink and ran down to see what was going on.

In the distance an ambulance moved up to the rubble that was once a bar. My thoughts then went to the bar owner and his daughter. I had only been acquainted with them for minutes, but I felt a real emptiness and pain that something may have happened to them.

We made our way back to the ship totally deflated. At the same time, the thought of what could have happened to us had we decided to have one more beer, didn't bear thinking about.

Life can take many twists and turns and in this case one simple decision and penchant for exploration, probably saved our lives. John always said if I had stayed he would have been quite happy spending the afternoon there.

We were leaving for Pathos the next morning and were desperate for news about the casualties. I quizzed the ship's agent and he said he understood two people were badly injured and were rushed by helicopter to a hospital in Nicosia.

I have never been really religious but I said a little prayer that night.

Hassan the scouser

Our next port of call was Beirut. In the early sixties it was a beautiful cosmopolitan city, known by many as the Paris of the Middle East. The city was the focal point of the region's cultural life. Theatres, restaurants and nightlife that could compete with Europe's finest. It is the capital and largest city in Lebanon and it played a central role in the country's economy.

On our arrival, the port was congested and we had to anchor and wait for an empty berth. The harbour was a hive of activity as the ship slowly drifted around to the nearest free buoy. The Arab boatmen secured our forward ropes to the buoy, then made their way to the after end to secure the rear ropes. The chief cook and I, taking a well-earned tea break, leaned on the rail watching the small, motorised boat towing the heavy ropes towards the vacant buoy. We scanned around to take in the atmosphere and although it was early morning, the temperature was already in the high eighties. It was good to spend a few minutes away from the heat of the galley. What stood out for me though was the backdrop that the Lebanese Mountains provided. Although it was hot, they were beautifully capped with snow. The bright blue sky and snow capped mountains painted an enchanting frame around the bustling harbour.

Raised Arabic voices from the small motorboat guided our eyes back to the men. One was pointing to the after end of our ship and shouting, almost screaming. We looked down at the churning water, pumped up by the screw as we maneuvered into position. A grey bloated body was being tossed around as if in a large washing machine. The shouts caught the attention of the bridge and the engines were immediately shut down. All hands descended on the poop deck to see what the fuss was about. The boatmen then made their way to the body and tried to secure it with a long boathook. What happened next was quite unexpected and totally sickening. As they tugged at the body the stomach split open disgorging blackened entrails into the sea. I almost threw up; it was a terrible sight to witness. Ship to shore radio was used to call the port health authority and within half an hour they retrieved the body as best they could and secured it in a body bag. Not a nice job. We were told a couple of days later that it was the body of a 19-year-old lad that had been swimming in the harbour six weeks previously. He had been reported missing. It was assumed he had got into difficulties and had become entangled in underwater debris. The turning over of the propeller had disturbed the body and sent it to the surface.

The next day a berth became vacant and we went alongside. During the day one of the ship's junior officers or apprentices manned the gangway, to check everybody coming aboard and keep any undesirables off. After 8pm the company employed a night watchman, a local. His duties included waking everyone up in the morning, officers and crew alike, ensuring they had time for breakfast before going on watch. We got to know one of the regular watchmen quite well. After visiting Beirut on a two monthly basis, he had cultured a really great party piece. Not only could he speak very good English, he could talk in five dialects, Cockney, Brummie, Scouser, Geordie and Glaswegian. He was short in stature and quite a rotund jovial character, every bit Arabic in appearance; he was probably in his late fifties. The Liverpool crew knew him as Hassan the Scouser. No doubt a similar nickname for Cockneys etc. As we were going ashore he greeted me and said "Alright cook have ya left me some sarnies in the mess room?" I joked, "Yes, your favourite - pork". He flung an imaginary punch at me and said, "Bring us back a bevvie!" He was so funny and had an answer for everything. He could carry on a conversation with three different members of the crew all seamlessly speaking different dialects and switch dialects as he spoke. It was quite an art to witness.

In the early hours of the morning about five of us returned back on board to find the gangway unattended, Hassan was nowhere to be seen. We looked through the porthole to see him fast asleep on the mess room table. He was surrounded by empty cans of beer, probably given to him by members of the crew. We decided to play a trick on Hassan; first we covered him with a Union Jack, and then turned the mess room clock foreword to half past seven. Next door, in the greaser's mess, the clock was also altered.

We watched through a porthole as one of the lads threw an empty can onto the floor beside him. Startled he woke up, in the same instant his eyes widened as he stared with an incredulous look at the clock on the bulkhead. *"Oh Oh Oh*

Oh" he spluttered, running still entangled in the Union Jack. The galley crew should have been called at 5.30. He raced into the next mess room and again checked the clock; screams of panic accompanied him on his route to wake up sleeping crewmates. We then realised he was taking a shortcut to the upper decks to wake up the Officers. It was now our time to panic as he was headed towards the Chief Officer's door. We scrambled up after him and managed to stop him in his tracks. Boy, was he mad! He ranted on at us in an unrecognized mixture of Scouse, Arabic and Cockney, punctuated with expletives. Unfortunately all the commotion caused alleyway doors to open and we were all ordered to report to the Captain in the morning. We retired to the mess room to calm down Hassan and concoct a story that would keep Hassan in work and prevent him from being fired for sleeping on the Job.

The story we decided upon and stuck to was that two of the crew had decided to play a prank on Hassan by changing the clocks. In order to do that they had to create a diversion so they could gain access to the mess rooms. One of the lads, after returning, tripped and went sprawling into the scuppers in the outside alleyway. Hassan went to his aid and while his attention was diverted, one of the able seamen changed the clocks. We drew straws to decide which of us would carry the can.; the idea being only two would be fined and the rest of us would contribute to allay costs. This was preferred to all of us being charged. I was lucky on that occasion, as I was not picked. Hassan was still angry and it was a time before he could get his tongue in gear and produce the correct accent again. He then agreed to go along with our tale, as it would free him from the responsibility of sleeping on the Job.

The next day we clubbed together and bought him a watch. That and 200 cigarettes made him the same happy Hassan we had all come to love. To a man we felt guilty that Hassan the scouser could have lost his job. I made many more trips to Beirut and it was always a pleasure to find Hassan was our night watchman.

Chapter Three – Animal Antics

Grass monkey

As I mentioned earlier, one of my favourite runs was down the South American coast, calling at Brazil, Uruguay and Argentina. The company I sailed with was Houlder Brothers. I must have been almost 17 years old at the time and still wet behind the ears but finding the South American run wild and exciting. A typical trip would be, Liverpool - Cape Verde Islands for bunkers (fuel) then across the southern Atlantic to Rio De Janeiro - Recife - Santos - Montevideo - Buenos Aires. Then back up the Brazilian coast stopping at one or two ports on the way home then returning to Liverpool. The ships were well appointed and mainly crewed by Liverpool seamen. Trips lasted six to eight weeks then possibly ten days in Liverpool loading and back out again. They were always happy ships and men were often reluctant to leave.

This story begins in the Cape Verde Islands; aboard a ship called "*Oswestry Grange*". Notices posted in the mess rooms

The Oswestry Grange

had warned us that monkeys were not allowed on board as pets. I had no intention of buying one until I saw the cutest monkey being ill-treated by one of the vendors. It was a small Grass Monkey and I watched as it cowered every time the seller so much as looked at it, he back handed it a couple of times. I argued with him and he said if he didn't sell it, he would kill it when he leaves the ship. I found out later this was a ploy used to get young, naive lads like me to buy the monkeys thinking they would save them from death. Anyway, being an animal lover, I fell for it hook, line and sinker. I haggled with him and was soon parted with my hard-earned cash, becoming the proud owner of Monty, whom I named after one of the engineers.

This particular engineer used to do gymnastics on deck with such fluidity he had been nicknamed "*Monkey*". I had no intention in keeping Monty, my aim was to get him to the South American coast without detection and hopefully sell him recuperating my outlay. I stupidly believed I was saving its life! I hid him in my cabin for a few days and gradually all in my alleyway became aware of my secret stowaway. We moved Monty around during inspection, keeping one-step ahead of the inspection party. Although I kept my cabin spotlessly clean, it was difficult to hide the monkey smell, so just prior to inspection my cabin was awash with Old Spice after-shave lotion to try and cover all traces. Our cabins all backed on to an outside alleyway, one of the deck-boys ran from porthole to porthole, passing Monty around ahead of the inspection party. Unfortunately, my cabin smelt like a brothel with large doses of Yardley's and Old Spice. As the inspection party entered my cabin the captain said, "*Jesus laddie have you got a woman in here, it smells like a whore's bedroom*?" I chuckled to myself, as I wondered where he had occasion to smell a whore's bedroom! "*It's no laughing matter laddie take it easy on the after-shave, don't overdo it I can see you take care of your cabin, there's no need*". I thought, oh if only you knew.

We would exercise Monty on a long chain between the hatches, away from the officers' eyes. By now most of the crew below officer level were aware of Monty and all played a part in concealing him. That was until one day, when one of the stewards after a drinking binge the night before thought he would give Monty a bit more freedom, he let him off his chain. Off he went, up and down masts and derricks, pursued by half the crew. We had no chance of catching him; he then headed off in the direction of the officers' accommodation. Some of the lads gave up the chase, not willing to face the consequences as I clambered the decks in pursuit midships. I saw Monty's tail disappear into the Captains open porthole.

Unfortunately the Captain was having a late morning nap after being up most of the night owing to fog. Monty bounded across the Captains chest rudely awakening him. Strong expletives escaped the porthole and within ten minutes I was ordered to report to the bridge. The Captain hastily dressed and it was obvious he was not a happy man. I was read the riot act; fined four days pay and told that this was not the end of the matter. He informed me he would have to put Monty overboard, as he could not risk taking him into Rio because the company was liable to be fined. I pleaded with him to spare Monty.

The bosun informed me they were getting dunnage (inexpensive or waste material used to load and secure cargo during transportation) from one of the hatches to make Monty a raft. Two deckhands and the bosun had been assigned to build it. Sure enough out on deck they were strapping dunnage together. I was raging they couldn't do this to a helpless animal. I stormed onto deck to confront the perpetrators. They wouldn't listen to reason, so I started throwing pieces of dunnage over the side and in my anger I even hurled some of the tools into the sea. As they grappled to stop me, they burst into laughter and admitted to me that it was all just a wind up.

The Captain allowed me to keep Monty with the promise I would endeavour to sell him, or find a home for him on the South American coast. Unfortunately, before I was able to do so, Monty came to a tragic end. He was attacked and killed by large rats in a port called Rosario in the upper reaches of the River Plate. We were on a berth aptly named 'rat wharf'. The wharf was completely overrun with rats, so much so that a drum was placed on top of the gangway, full of 3ft lengths of heavy bamboo cane. The purpose of the cane was that any crew going ashore would take a cane to ward of rats when they left the ship, deposit the cane at a drum by the dock gates, then collect one on the way back to the ship. This became a sport for some of the crew who totted up how many rats they manage to kill on the half a mile jaunt ashore. At night, the rats seemed to overrun the quayside; it was like a scene from the Pied Piper. Early one afternoon Monty was having his usual exercise on a running chain between the hatches. One of the sailors found him lying dead; his small body savaged by bite marks. It was determined the rats had managed to get on board despite rat guards on the ship's ropes. I was devastated, having become very attached to that mischievous bundle of fun.

I cringe now when I think how I had been taken in first by the vendor then by the crew, but looking back, episodes like this are all building blocks that teach us lessons in life and mould us into what we become; hopefully wiser and more sensible.

Kinkajou

I was on my way to South America on a PSNC ship, called The Sarmiento. It was the first time and only time that I joined a ship with my friend Wayne Yeates. It was a happy ship, most of the crew got along with each other. The usual tales of other trips and ports filled the recreation time.

MV Sarmieto PSNC

It was one of those evenings mid Atlantic that the word Kinkajou entered my vocabulary.

The Kinkajou (shown below) is a member of the Raccoon family, though many of its features and traits sound like those of a primate and it lives in the tropical forests of Central and South America, where they spend most of their time in the trees.

They are able to turn their feet backwards to run easily in either direction along branches or up and down trunks. The kinkajou also has a prehensile tail that it uses much like another arm. Kinkajou's often hang from this incredible tail, which also aids their balance and serves as a cosy blanket while the animal sleeps high in the canopy.

A Kinkajou

Kinkajous are sometimes called honey bears because they raid bees' nests. They use their long, skinny tongues to slurp honey from a hive and to remove insects like termites from their nests. The Kinkajou's diet includes fruit and small mammals, which they snare with their nimble front paws and sharp claws. They roam and eat at night and return each morning to sleep in previously used tree holes.

One of the stewards on the previous trip had bought a Kinkajou in Buenaventura Columbia. He spent a lot of time and energy painting glowing pictures of what fantastic pets they made.

His had become a family pet and his uncle was so taken by it he was under orders to bring another home. Being a lover of animals, I couldn't wait to hit the Columbian coast and seek out one of these loveable creatures for myself. We went alongside in Buenaventura and as soon as customs had cleared the ship, the usual bunch of traders alighted, spreading all manner goods and souvenirs on the canvas encased hatch covers. There were woodcarvings, butterfly trays, Columbian coffee, etc., even parrots, but alas no Kinkajous. I enquired at a bum boat, which is a boat selling goods from the side of the ship, where I may find one, "*Don't worry*" he said, "*I Mauricio will bring you one tomorrow, for you a very good price, because I like the English*". I thought, "*What a salesman*", knowing that this was the patter he would tailor to all nationalities that crossed his path.

The following day we were due to sail late afternoon. Time seemed to stand still as I waited patiently for Mauricio to arrive. It was almost time to pull up the gangway and I surmised he had let me down. Then I spotted him running out from between the sheds. He had what appeared to be a huge coconut type shell. To this day, I don't know what type of shell it was, but it had been split in half and tied together with a lot of string. Inside was, he said, my Kinkajou. I handed over three US Dollars, which in those days, especially in Columbia was quite a lot of money. As I took the shell from him, it seemed to have a life of its own. Frantic movement from inside accompanied by a sharp scratching sound, as the inhabitant fought to find a way out. Mauricio informed me the kinkajou was a timid creature and that it would be very scared. He told me not to open it yet, but to let it settle down for half an hour, then slowly release it into my cabin giving it time to acclimatise. I look back now and think how naive I was. Yes, you've guessed it! I couldn't wait half an hour. Ten minutes later, I was busy untying the very tight knots. The scurrying inside was getting quite frantic. As the shell parted and obviously frightened and angry creature bared its sharp fangs and jumped at my face. I fell over backwards dropping the empty shell. The terrified animal quickly retreated under my bunk. Armed with a blanket as protection, I managed to contain the racoon-like animal and place it back in the shell. I was to find out later my three dollars had actually purchased a coati mundi.

When provoked, or for defence, coatis can be fierce fighters; their strong jaws, sharp canine teeth and fast scratching paws, along with a tough hide sturdily attached to the underlying muscles, make it very difficult for potential predators (e.g., dogs or jaguars) to seize the smaller mammal. Source: *Wikipedia, the free encyclopaedia*

Coati Mundi

I ran out on deck, just as the ship was pulling away from the quayside. Mauricio had long gone, leaving me with an animal I had no inclination to try to tame. We were now bound for our next port. The next few days and a few bites and nasty scratches later, I decided I could not tame the coati mundi. I had tried to persevere and make friends with my bad tempered lodger! Although I managed to feed it, the aggressive behaviour continued. I took to wearing leather gloves as protection given to me by the bosun. The crew thought the whole episode was hilarious. I needed to get rid in the next port of call.

Further down the coast, we called into Guayaquil in Ecuador, the area around the docks had a notoriously wild reputation. Still wondering what to do with my ferocious cabin mate, I joined some of my Liverpool shipmates ashore in the Skandi Bar. There seemed to be one in every port on the South American coast. The bar lay a short distance from the harbour, catering mainly for seaman. For many it was a first port of call, an ideal watering place as you made your way up the hot dusty streets to explore the area. It was a real sleazy joint. Walking in from the harsh sunshine your eyes take a moment to adjust to the almost night-time darkness. A huge cockroach made a crunching noise as I inadvertently stood on it. Flags of every nation hung on the walls. Football banners from all over the world were suspended from wooden ceiling joists. In pride of place, behind the ancient till, hung a Liverpool football club scarf and a dog-eared faded picture of Bill Shankly. It was open twenty-three hours a day and only closed for one hour at 5am, mainly to brush and swill the floor. That hour also served to remove any inebriated seamen. They were unceremoniously propped up against the wall outside to await collection from any returning shipmates. Fresh sawdust was then spread on the floor. The sawdust helped mop up any blood as many a drunken seaman fought in honour of his nationality, football team, women, or any other raft of silly excuses. We drank beer and sang Beatles songs, as the ladies of the day or night tried to split up our party and ply their trade in some dingy bedroom at the rear of the bar.

At one end of the bar was a kitchen of sorts. The barman was beating a huge T Bone steak with an old beer bottle; he threw it onto a greasy hotplate that didn't look as if it had been cleaned in months. No thought was given to hygiene, but the lads who succumbed said it was the best steak they had ever tasted - didn't say much for our cooking! I must admit things got rather rowdy as the English and the Germans tried to out-sing each other. The local women sang along to the Beatles songs in their broken English. Beatle fame had made a huge impact even in this far-flung part of the world. This annoyed the Germans as the women left their tables to join in the latest Beatle Hits.

Wayne and I decided to move on. We ambled up the hot almost empty streets into town to have a look around. Within an hour we had seen all of interest in this dusty outpost, so we made our way back to the bar, at least it was lively there. In those days, Wayne loved his beer. Lively it certainly was! As we entered the bar, tables, chairs and bodies were flying everywhere. Our lads were taking a beating, so we waded in to try to calm things down. It turned out trouble had started when the lads started singing Liverpool Football Songs. The Germans reacted by singing German football songs, the war was mentioned, insults on both sides exchanged.

We managed to pull some of the brawlers apart, but one particularly large ugly member of the opposition still wanted to fight the world. To ward him off one of the bartenders, who looked like he could go ten rounds with Mohamed Ali, grabbed an evil-looking boning knife from behind the bar. The loud-mouthed unruly thug picked up a barstool and lunged at the barman. In his drunken, maniacal state, he went sprawling across the sawdust floor and head first into the old iron grease-encrusted stove. This seemed to have done the trick, as he lay quiet for some minutes. Eventually he groggily rose to his feet, blood streaming from a head wound, the hate-filled expletives started again. He turned his attention to me, accusing me of hitting him with a stool while his back was turned. The remaining Germans tried to calm him down, explaining what had happened, Wayne and another of the ships crew intervened. Punches again traded and it looked as though it was going to flare up again. Some of the bargirls, trying to diffuse the situation, fed the ancient American jukebox and started sexily dancing to Latin American music, between the opposing sides. This deflated the tension and things calmed down.

One of our lads told the drunken aggressor that I had bought a Kinkajou in the last port, but that I wasn't allowed keep it. With a sudden interest, he approached me, and was suddenly my best friend; he asked if I would sell it to him. I sold it to him for five dollars using the same tactics Mauricio had used on me. I tied the knots on the shell as tightly as possible and left the handover until just before they raised the gangway. I felt pangs of guilt about the deal, but had he been a nicer person it would have been different. I am afraid it was dog eat dog. The last I saw of him was a waving fist from the deck of his ship as we passed on the way to our next port.

On our way to Valparaiso we called in at many ports, I kept my eyes open for that German freighter, as it was normal for the ships on that run to frequent the same ports.

I managed to buy a kinkajou in the next port, Iquique, in Chile, a real cute mischievous pet that I named Jeremy. What I didn't know at the time was that kinkajous are nocturnal. He really came alive at night. I spent the next few weeks trying to change his sleeping habits, all to no avail. Although at night Jeremy occupied a large latched cupboard beneath my bunk, he would manage to find a way out and I'd wake to find the cabin in a mess. Toothpaste tubes squeezed, towels, all over the place, he even succeeded in opening drawers. One time he managed to tear apart a feather pillow. After his rampage, he

Sister Lynne with Jeremy the Kinkajou

would cuddle up alongside me with his large prehensile tail wrapped around one of my arms.

We had two other kinkajous on board. On sunny, pleasant days, they would scamper around one of the hatches together. There were numerous exotic birds on board, parrots, parakeets etc.; one guy even bought a boa constrictor. The Captain called a halt to any more purchases saying the ship was beginning to resemble Noah's Ark.

Things have changed so much now as in the sixties we had no problem bringing all manner of creatures into the British Isles. The only form I remember signing, was an agreement that I was not bringing Jeremy into contact with livestock or farm facilities.

I took Jeremy home and the family immediately encompassed and loved him. Dad built him a large cage to curtail his night-time activities. Unfortunately he always found a way out. Mornings were spent clearing up the mess, turning off taps, seeking out where he hid the bathroom toiletries, rolling up toilet paper, etc. Mum became rather annoyed by it all and said if we could not train it, it would have to go. Jeremy had such a cuddly and loveable nature; he was now part of the family.

Another name that the kinkajou is commonly known as is "*Honey Bear*" and thereby lays an hilarious story.

Bob and Eileen Roberts, our closest family friends lived about a mile from us. I had promised to take Jeremy around to their house, as Eileen couldn't wait to see him. It was a very chilly morning and a couple of inches of overnight snow covered the ground. I was wearing a brand new cream jacket that I had bought in Panama. With Jeremy being a tropical creature I thought it best to keep his feet away from the cold snow. I carried him; another one of my many mistakes in life! Jeremy decided to discharge his last meal down the front of my favourite new jacket! What a mess! I gingerly took of my jacket managing to clean most off the mess. I then turned the jacket inside out and threw it over my arm. Can you imagine what I must have looked like? On a freezing cold morning, jacket off and flung over my arm a white shirt and a strange animal on a lead bouncing and skipping through the snow. I still had a mile to walk, in quite a rough area. Believe me I got some strange looks. As for Jeremy, he loved the snow and all he wanted to do was frolic. He didn't seem to notice the cold at all.

Gar and Barbara related this next story to me, on my return from a short voyage.

It seems one morning Jeremy had escaped from his cage and was nowhere to be seen, the house was searched from top to bottom. The question was asked, "*How had he escaped*?" all doors were locked, all windows closed! After he was missing for a few hours, Barbara and Sandra, who were both still young children, aged 10 and 11, were absolutely distraught and they reported the missing animal to the local police station. Barbara said to the desk sergeant, with tears streaming down her face, "*Our bear has es*caped" The sergeant didn't believe her and asked her to describe it. "*It's a golden brown colour with a long tail*", she said. "*Don't be daft replied the sergeant, bears don't have long tails*". "*Ours does*" replied the girls in unison. By now, another police officer had joined the conversation. Barbara and Sandra got the impression that rather than take them seriously, the laughing police officers were treating it all as a joke and were just humouring them.

They took down details of the animal and their address and said, "*Well, if anybody finds your bear... with a long tail...we will be in touch*". As they left the station, the girls could hear the laughter in the background.

Later on that day after returning from work, Gar joined in the search. As the evening darkened, he decided to have one last look in the back garden. Scanning the garden, rustling the bushes, he just happened to glance up. Running along the ridge tiles, he spotted Jeremy. He seemed to disappear over the roof to the front of the house. Gar ran through the narrow entry to the front. The entry separated the row of houses. Jeremy was nowhere to be seen. Returning to the back garden, Jeremy reappeared perched on a 4ft tall accessible wall. Moving slowly and deftly, Gar managed to grab Jeremy and contain him. Jeremy was completely covered in soot, so we decided that he must have escaped via our chimney. We wondered how many other chimneys he had negotiated.

Imagine the neighbours' surprise to find a soot-ridden creature emerging from the fireplace! That evening Jeremy made the headlines in the local Liverpool Echo *'Bear on the loose in South Liverpool'.*

Jeremy became a liability and unfortunately, whilst I was away mum assessed that he was often neglected. In short, Jeremy had tried mum's patience. She said it was hard enough looking after six kids, without the liability of a bear, which came lively and mischievous when everyone was sleeping and in the process wrecking the house! Mum decided enough was enough he had to go. I tried to argue the case, but was told *"It's okay for you! You will be off to sea in a few days time; you don't have to clear the mess up!"*

It was with great reluctance I sold Jeremy to a pet shop for £5 and they assured me they would find it a good caring home. Jennifer, Sandra and Barbara were inconsolable, Jennifer, the eldest of the three tried to buy him back hours later but was informed that Jeremy was already re-housed.

We decided that the shop didn't want to sell it back, because the price they had paid, was a lot less than the valuation of £50 to £60 we obtained after the fact. I was not flavour of the month for many weeks after and I've since been informed that I'm still not flavour of the century!

On reflection, I should have researched the background and habits of the Kinkajou, but in those days, we didn't have the Internet to guide us. How easy everything is for this generation!

A bit rough around here

I was working for the shipping company T. J. Harrison, taking the MV Barrister around the land. We were standing in for the ship's crew while they took their leave. We left Liverpool, first calling at Swansea, then onto the West India dock in London. In those days, shipping cargo around the coast was a cheaper option than road transport; motorways were rare in the early sixties.

MV Barrister

On our first evening in London, Bill, the second steward and I decided to explore the area around the docks. As we descended the gangway, the ship's watchman shouted after us, "*Be careful lads it's a bit rough around here*". We walked for a while and ended up in Bethnal Green. We saw a pub called "*The Rising Sun*", which was absolutely packed with people, to the point that some drinkers had over spilled onto on the pavements. We went in to see what the attraction was. Over at one end of the smoke filled room a pianist played in accompaniment for anyone who cared to sing.

We fought our way to the bar and ordered two pints of lager. We managed to find a seat and sipped our drinks, just taking in the atmosphere. After a couple more pints I felt a little inebriated - it didn't take much for me! I was never a drinker. Bill challenged me to sing. "No chance" I said. He offered to pay my round. This I could not resist, as he was well known for having the dustiest wallet on the ship! A couple of beers later I agreed to the deal, made sure he got the next round in and made my way to the piano. I decided to sing House of the Rising Sun changing the words to suit the venue.

There is a house in Bethnal Green they call the Rising Sun
It's been the ruin of many a poor boy and God I know, I'm one
My mother was a tailor she sewed my new blue jeans
My father was a gamblin' man down in Bethnal Green

It seemed to be going down quite well. It was so noisy I thought they were cheering me, then out of the noise filtered the baying crowd as they shouted:

"*Get him off, off off off*", *Rubbish!*, *Boo,boo, boooo, Leave him alone he's enjoying himself*". Halfway through my rendition I took the hint and left the stage. That's when I got the loudest cheer. I must have been absolutely awful! My so-called mate was helpless with laughter; he said, "*That round was worth every penny*!" After a few hours, and a little bit worse-for-wear with hunger setting in, we started to make our way back to the ship.

A low-lying freezing fog added to the drabness of West India Dock Road. Pulsating through the fog a flashing neon sign advertised a Chinese Restaurant. We quickened our step to seek out food and warmth. Once inside we discovered it was quite tacky and tired, in obvious need of a little care and attention. It also sported one of my pet hates; a carpet that was so greasy, it seemed to suck at your feet each step you took. Nevertheless, we were so hungry it was not a time to get fussy and despite all its shortcomings, it was very busy. The food must be good, I thought. We queued and waited for a table. The oriental aromas from the kitchen and the clashing of pans, accompanied by raised foreign voices only enhanced our hunger. It was obvious that they were short staffed.

The young pretty waitress looked quite dishevelled as she buzzed between the tables, as diners from all around vied for her attention. Eventually we were guided to a table right in the centre of the restaurant. After what seemed an age, our meal was served. I had ordered special fried rice, Bill had ordered a chicken curry and we had decided to share. We didn't get a chance; an explosion of glass penetrated the noisy restaurant. I looked up to see one of the restaurant windows showering the fleeing, screaming diners. A gang of heavies burst in with baseball bats and set about smashing everything. All around customers fled their tables. The restaurant emptied. They smashed mirrors and light-fittings, tables and chairs as they hurled them across the room. The bar and its contents were destroyed as we sat glued in our seats, transfixed and open mouthed, spoon and fork still poised, as everything around us was totally wrecked. We were in total shock.

I think they left us alone because we were just young lads. It was all over in minutes. They calmly walked out single file and with one last strike, they smashed a large pottery Chinese dragon as they left. Ours was the only table left with legs, although somehow our meals had merged with the heavily patterned carpet. It looked as though a bomb had exploded; there was nothing to salvage, except our two chairs and one table! The owners who turned out to be Vietnamese were hysterical. One of the kitchen staff had to be restrained as he attempted to follow them brandishing a broken table leg. I felt sorry for one of the cooks as I watched him. He sat in the middle of the carnage with his head in his hands moaning repeatedly.

"Everything finish", *"Everything finish"*, *"Everything finish"*.

The owner's young daughter, who had served us only moments before, was shaking and in shock. She told us that the assailants were local gangsters after protection money.

The ship's watchman was correct... it was rough.

Not you again!

Late the next afternoon the official ship's crew re-joined the vessel. After the handover we set off for Euston railway station to catch a late evening train back to Liverpool. Arriving at Euston nearing midnight we had to settle for what was called the milk run. That was a train that stopped at every station dropping off mail and newspapers at each point along the way. It was an eight-hour journey. Unable to afford a sleeper, I settled for buying a stack of magazines and newspapers at the station shop. Armed with plenty to read boredom would have no time to settle in.

Just north of Watford I turned a page in a magazine type paper called '*Reveille*'. For a heart-stopping moment, I sat there shocked and entranced. There in front of me was an uncanny drawing of a little wizened old man. It was the same one that I had seen in my bedroom all those years ago as a child. I stared in disbelief. He was exactly as I remembered him. Old and wrinkled, without legs and that wicked grin on his face. I quickly scanned the story. Huyton, Liverpool, children, laughing, wrinkled, silent, no legs. All the key clues backed up my story. I read it over and over again as a chill ran through my body. The story was based in Burtree Road in Huyton, not a road that I was familiar with, but at the time, I was only a child. Well, I was certainly not bored now. I couldn't wait to get home to reveal my findings to my mother. The night dragged on, I tried to read other material, but was continually drawn back to those pages over and over again.

It seemed a little girl was playing in an upstairs bedroom, her father doing a spot of DIY downstairs. He heard a number of ear piercing screams, followed by a large bang. He ran upstairs calling his daughters name, but there was no answer. He attempted to open the bedroom door to find a large wardrobe blocking his way. It was so heavy he had to recruit the assistance of a neighbour to help him to gain access. It turned out that the little girl was playing with her dolls, when she felt a presence behind her. As she turned, she witnessed an apparition of the little old man without legs, silently laughing at her. She screamed and panicking, ran for the door. As if by magic the large wardrobe moved across the floor blocking her exit. She passed out in shock. The family moved out and another unsuspecting household moved in, where reports told of a little boy who twice saw the old man on the stairs. Terrified they too moved out. The article stated that nobody wanted to live there, the house stood empty for many years.

I caught a taxi at Lime Street station in a rush to get home. With no time for pleasantries, I blurted out "Read this". I watched as the colour drained from my mother's face, "*Oh my God*" she said, "*Our house was haunted*" "*Where's Burtree Road*?" I asked. "*That was the road next to ours*" she replied.

There was no easy way to get from Speke to Huyton, so with no expense spared we ordered a taxi. On arrival, we found that the empty house in question backed straight on to Seacroft Close. To this day, I find it hard to reconcile a belief in ghosts, but I cannot explain what else it could have been.

Chapter Four - Deceived

A short trip?

Early 1965 I called at The Maritime office on Mann Island, at Liverpool Pier Head. I was looking for a short voyage after doing three quite long trips. I was offered the MV Cape Wrath, 10660 gross tonnage capable of 14 knots on what is called round the land UK and over to Sweden and back. In all we were told that it should be no longer than six weeks.

I joined the Cape Wrath in Birkenhead on a grey, wet morning. Derricks were swinging back and forth unloading wet pallets of cargo. The ship looked equally miserable and I felt glad it was to be a short trip. I struggled up the slippery gangway with a large, battered, travel-weary case. A galley boy who was having a smoke and mug of tea on deck, greeted me and showed me to my cabin. I deposited my case, after quick wash to freshen up; I made my way to the galley to meet the chief cook.

MV Cape Wrath

First impressions were not good. A rather unkempt, unshaven character sporting a blood soaked dirty apron greeted me. He slurred without removing the ash-laden cigarette from his mouth "*Just made some tea do you want one?*" He reached to the metal ledge. A mug appeared containing a set of false teeth in a substance that looked like bleach. As he took the teeth out I hastily declined, *"No thanks...just had lunch"*. My first conversation with him was a lie. Although I was parched, I could not face the prospect of drinking from that mug. *"Suit yourself"*, he said reaching for his tobacco tin. Spitting the remains of his cigarette butt into the sand bucket outside the galley door, he started to roll another. I made a mental note to look after my own food and drink from then on.

I was glad to find the cook was only temporary, as he was waiting for a replacement. He had been given his marching orders for unhygienic practices. I was thrown in at the deep end. The cook gave me the dinner menu and promptly retired to his cabin with a case of beer.

View from Birkenhead to the Pier Head Liverpool

I sought out the galley boy and we spent the next hour scrubbing and trying to swill down the galley. The drains were completely blocked. We discovered later that, as a leaving present, the exiting chief cook had poured a vat of hot lard down the scuppers blocking the drains in the galley. The engineers had to remove some pipes under the galley to clear the blockage. We then prepared the meal. That evening we worked late into the early hours, clearing out the fridges, scrubbing the duckboards and shelving and dumping food that had long passed its sell by date. I wondered how things had deteriorated to this degree, with the scrupulous inspections that usually take place on a weekly basis.

The next two days I spent working on-board, the outgoing cook never made an appearance, preferring to spend his time drinking and playing cards until he was paid off. The new chief cook joined us two hours before sailing. A nice, clean and well-ordered galley greeted him. Most of the crew seemed quite friendly so I then signed on. In those days, we had to sign two years articles no matter what length the trip. I signed on as Second Cook and Baker with a monthly pay of £54.0s.10d with the promise of two and a half hours overtime a day. The overtime was good news to me; it made a huge difference to very poor pay. I sent a monthly allotment of £24 home to help out with family finances.

Later that afternoon we slipped our moorings and leaving Birkenhead docks, we entered the River Mersey. Visibility was poor due to the adverse weather, the ship rocked around a bit as it fought to make its way into the main shipping lane.

Leaving Liverpool always held a touch of sadness, even to hardened seafarers. A burst of torrential rain meant the Liver Buildings on the Pier Head soon disappeared into the mist.

Only the foghorns of nearby vessels broke the eerie silence that accompanied us as the ship sliced its way through mist-laden waters. We encountered a cold damp mist and drizzle all the way out to *Point Lynas,* where we discharged the pilot. We were now bound for London, our first port of call.

It was a mixed crew, Glasgow, Tyneside, Liverpool and South Wales being the main providers. All seemed quite friendly. Most had joined on the understanding that we were on a six-week voyage at most. One chap was due to be married in eight weeks time and it became apparent that all of the crew had been promised a good overtime package, so at that point we had a happy ship.

In the evenings we played cards and cribbage or listened to the bosun's short wave radio in the mess room. Some of the lads started losing money they had not yet earned. Newly found friends spent hours chatting about various ships and companies they had sailed with. Beer was in full flow from the recently issued stores. As the evening turned into the early hours there seemed to be a competition as to who could tell the most interesting tale and exaggeration came to the fore but slowly we all drifted away to our various cabins. I had to be up at 5.30 to prepare for the day ahead.

Press ganged

Just south of Lands End, everything seemed great, the crew were getting to know each other and forming friendships. There was a general good feeling with the thought of a happy, short trip. The mood changed as respective heads of departments informed us that there was a last minute change of orders, our first port of call was now to be Tampa in Florida to pick up a cargo for Ocean Island in the Pacific Ocean. We would then load Phosphate bound for New Zealand. This did not go down well, most of the crew started showing signs of unrest and the underlying belligerence soon turned to anger as they felt they had been deceived. The "*short trip*" story seemed to be a means of getting a crew to sign on, knowing the shipping company could tie the crew to a 2-year contract once we had left British waters.

In bygone days, they used a press gang to make up the crew in area shortages; this was just a different tactic. Nobody could speculate how long this voyage would last; from now on, we were at the mercy of Lyle Shipping Company. The general feeling was that knowledge had been stifled as the company men on board would certainly have known of these tactics and probably had prior knowledge of our itinerary. The type of voyage we had unwittingly signed onto was known as *tramping. Signing two-year articles was compulsory in the sixties and no matter what company you signed with you had no other option but to agree. We had to just get on with it and hope that after New Zealand we would return home.

A ship engaged in the tramp trade is one that does not have a fixed schedule or published ports of call. As opposed to freightliners, tramp ships trade on the spot market with no fixed schedule or itinerary/ports-of-call(s). A Steam ship engaged in the tramp trade is sometimes called a tramp trader the similar terms tramp freighter and "tramper" are also in use. The term is derived from the British meaning of "tramp" as itinerant beggar or vagrant; in this context it is first documented in the 1880s, along with "ocean tramp" (at the time many sailing vessels engaged in irregular trade as well).
Source: *Wikipedia, the free encyclopaedia*

Bless the loaves

The chief steward who was known by the nickname of JC informed the catering staff that he had cut all overtime. This was announced after only one week of departure. Mine was cut from two and a half hours to half an hour a day. Not only were we saddled with a much longer trip, we also had to accept less pay. Conditions changed overnight. The crew became angry and ill tempered; drinking, squabbling and fighting became the norm. What was an amicable crew became fragmented and clans began to form. As a young 18-year-old lad I felt particularly vulnerable and didn't want to get involved with all that was going on. I started to lock my cabin door at night, spent my time reading and listening to my short wave radio. Sometimes the fighting would spill out from the mess rooms to the alleyways. The next morning we would often have to clean blood from the bulkheads.

Our first Port of call was the Cape Verde Islands for bunkers (re-fuelling) to get us across the Atlantic Ocean. These were quite barren islands off the coast of Africa and duty free, so it made sense to bunker there. Six hours later, we headed off towards Tampa, Florida. After a week, the chief steward ordered us to cut back on stores, rationing the size of portions and joints of meat. Less meat meant I had to bake more bread to keep the crew from going hungry. In a meeting with the chief steward, he told me that I was using too much flour. I protested that the crew needed feeding and as they were getting smaller portions, they were eating more bread. His answer... "*I'm not asking you to cut the number of loaves just make them smaller*". This was an impossible situation, which caused conflict between the crew and galley staff. This in turn created bad feelings and made our lives very difficult. The job then became a real chore and a cloud hung over us from morning until night. In a short space of time, the atmosphere had changed completely.

There were rumours that certain crewmembers were making money out of the ships stores by conducting illegal arrangements with the ship chandlers; wheeling and dealing with ship supplies. Rumour was that they made quite a bit of money splitting the difference. This was never proven, so we will have to take it as rumour.

We used to say, "*JC has blessed the loaves*" hence the nickname.

Another nickname that was used throughout the Merchant Navy was a term applied behind the chief stewards back, "*belly robber*", an insulting term that was universal when feelings ran deep at the lack of quantity of food. But the galley staff took the full brunt as arguments festered throughout the mess rooms and at the galley door. We were between the devil and the deep blue sea, hit from both sides.

A lucky escape

The Cape Wrath docked in Tampa Florida. We seemed to be miles from anywhere, so after lunch, I had two hours off and a few of us decided to head out to a small beach that we had noticed while coming into port.

It was a beautiful beach, but surprisingly quiet. The sand was soft and fine and the weather was such that it was also very hot making walking on it akin to walking on hot coals. Not being a strong swimmer, I relaxed in warm clear waters close to the shoreline. After half an hour I edged into deeper water, making sure my feet kept contact with the seabed. A strong wave hit me taking my feet from under me. Unable to regain contact, the strong current started pushing me out into deeper waters. Panic set in as I fought the strong current, striking out for shore to no avail. I could feel myself being forced out to a headland across the bay. Being low in the water my friends disappeared from sight. My arms and legs were becoming leaden and I was tiring quickly with all the effort. Swallowing mouthfuls of incredibly salty seawater, made me panic even more. Incredibly, I knew that if I continued to panic, the end would come very quickly; I knew I had to rest. I decided to float, lying on my back to conserve energy. I was hoping the current would push me closer to the headland ahead.

My life flashed before me. What a way to go, so far from home with no goodbyes. I soon realised I was being drawn past the headland and into open seas. The survival instinct took over and I made one last desperate attempt to swim to the headland. It is amazing what reserves of energy you acquire when the odds are against you. About a quarter of a mile from the headland, my knee hit a boulder; I pushed myself forward to find my toes touching the bottom. Sharp coral pierced the soles of my feet; I lifted my legs and tried to half swim half float over it. My knees and hands became the target of the unrelenting coral. All this time the waves were buffeting me closer to the shore. I ended up on my forearms and knees crawling up the beach, with every movement adding to the wounds of my already lacerated body. I eventually reached soft sand and collapsed on the beach. Almost immediately, I became very cold and started violently shaking. This I believe was the effect of shock. Water was lapping at my body but I could not find the energy to move.

From the distance, I could hear voices filtering through the sound of the waves lapping up against my face. Raising my sand encrusted face and spotted two men running towards me. They had seen me from the top of the cliff struggling in the sea. One went back for a blanket, but it was an age before I could stop the convulsive shaking. After a short rest, they helped me up the rocks. They loaded me into a truck and took me back to the ship. My friends had reported me missing and feared I had drowned. They were about to report to the local coastguard, when the truck carrying me pulled up to the gangway.

For the first time on this trip, I was glad to be back on the Cape Wrath. The chief steward called the ship's agent who took me to the local hospital, where they treated my wounds and gave me a course of antibiotics. For the next three weeks, I was walking around like an Egyptian mummy. From then on I practiced swimming at every opportunity. However, to this day it's not one of my strong points, but I have learned my lesson and ever since I hug the shoreline.

Coral reefs are colonies of creatures with calcareous, or bony, exoskeletons that often feature sharp angles or ridges, so it's not uncommon for swimmers and divers to suffer lacerations after making contact with reefs. Once the skin has been broken, "Coral poisoning", characterised by raised, itchy red welts that develop as capillaries become inflamed, can set in within minutes. In addition to minor side effects like localised pain and a relatively low fever, coral poisoning may advance to Ulcerative Cellulites and sloughing of the skin around the wound, which can take as long as three to six weeks to heal. In rare but very serious cases, coral poisoning can lead to necrosis of the tissue surrounding the wound, ultimately resulting in sepsis or severe infection.
Source: *Wikipedia*

Madness

As the days passed, the general mood was worsening. Tempers would kick off at the slightest provocation. Some of the men were angry and disgruntled. They hadn't planned on being away so long, poor pay and conditions added to their grievance.

To get off the ship some of the men resorted to desperate and drink-fuelled crazy measures. It was so hot in the cabins with no air-conditioning and only blowers, which merely re-circulated the stale hot air. Cabin doors were left unlocked and ajar with only a door hook as a stay. One man, an ex submariner, suddenly seemed to suffer crazy spells. He began running up and down the accommodation alleyways, flipping the door hooks and kicking-in his fellow shipmates cabin doors. This became a nightly routine, usually in the early hours of the morning; manically laughing after each door burst open. It went on for a number of nights. Emotions ran high and it became too much for one able seaman, a big lad from South Wales, who waited for him, lying in his bunk with his foot poised on the other side of the door. As the maniac telegraphed his arrival he kicked open one door too many. As soon as he flipped the hook, the able seaman responded with an almighty kick to the door thereby trapping and breaking the lunatic's wrist. He was hospitalised and paid off in the next port. When they cleared his cabin, they found around fifty odd socks. They were all neatly hanging on pegs in his wardrobe. For weeks, most of the crew had been complaining they were losing one sock out of a pair, after hanging them in the alleyways to dry.

Another able seaman, forced into cancelling his wedding was desperate and quite inebriated. He stopped by the galley and demanded that the chief cook, hit his right hand with the back of a cleaver to render him unable to work, giving him the excuse to be paid off and sent home. The cook told him to get lost and not be so stupid.

A few more beers later, the man came back and pleaded once again with the chief cook. This went on throughout the afternoon. The cook was starting to get rather irritated by it all; the fact that he had also been drinking while working didn't help matters. He said to me, "*if that idiot comes back once more I'm going to do it*". I didn't believe for one minute he was serious and told him not to be so daft.

He came back once again stumbling and slurring expletives at the galley door, I tried to usher him back to his cabin. However, he was having none of it and got quite aggressive. The cook confronted him agreeing to do it, "*Come on you are all talk*", he said.   A rolled up tea towel was placed over the seaman's wrist to prevent any major laceration. After two attempts the able seaman kept moving his hand away at the last minute.

The cook in his wisdom, decided to move the back end of the cleaver higher up his wrist! What a way to sober up. The excruciating pain sent him spinning out of the galley and onto the afterdeck. As he went down, he hit his head on a winch housing which rendered him unconscious. I argued with the cook and he threateningly told me that if I said a word to anyone my life would not be worth living.   Our working relationship became very strained from then on. They put it down as a freak accident. He got his wish but I believe had to spend six weeks in hospital before being repatriated on another merchant ship. One of his shipmates received a letter from him four months later to say he had fully recovered and was now happily married.

That was his way of getting away from the prison that the Cape Wrath had become.

A lot to learn

The galley boy, a hardworking lad from Pontypridd, asked if he could boil his whites, tee shirts etc., on the galley stove. It was common practice for the catering staff to use the galley, after serving dinner, to dhobi, a seafaring term for washing clothes. I gave him permission and he went ahead. The galley stove was a huge oil burning stove and the top plates were divided in four steel sections, these were kept immaculate, to satisfy the two inspections each week. The normal thing was to boil and bleach the whites in an old steel cauldron, which was kept specifically for the job. What happened next defied belief. He seemingly placed his washing in a plastic bucket and put it onto the hot plates, then promptly left to make himself a mug of tea in the steward's mess room. All panic broke out as the smell of burning plastic and the hiss of steam permeated the alleyways. The chief cook screamed, "*What's going on in the galley?*" We both raced up the stairway to find steam filling the alleyway and the nauseating smell of burning plastic. What a mess, the melting plastic was running between the plates and running down the front of the stove. We spent the next eight hours closing down the ovens, stripping down the stove and cleaning the plates. The galley boy didn't live that down for a long time. His new nickname, "*Daffy Taffy*", stayed with him until payoff and knowing the shipping grapevine, the nickname followed him to his next ship.

Chapter Five – Pacific Bound

Feeding the mules

On leaving Tampa, we set sail for the Panama Canal to gain entrance to the Pacific Ocean. The cook persuaded a couple of gullible first trippers that if they saved galley slops and any food waste, such as potato peelings to feed the mules that pulled us through the locks, the mule handlers would give them nice souvenirs and even dollars to go ashore. The lads were taken in completely by this and for three days hoarded leftovers in their cabins. The whole crew kept up the charade, one seaman even pretended to steal one of the buckets, arranging of course to get himself caught in the act. From then on, the lad locked his cabin and after three days in a warm climate, the buckets started to smell. The Captain and Chief Engineer carrying out the weekly inspection were

The Panama Canal

also involved in the hoax. They told the lads that it was the only time that their cabins were allowed to smell a little bit whiffy, emphasising that the mule owners were very poor and any help you give to them would help foster good relations with the Panamanian people. Roll on Panama. *"I've taken to sleeping out on deck, can't stand the smell*!" one of the unsuspecting deck lads said to me. Imagine their shock and disappointment when the *mules turned out to be locomotives.

Mules (mulas) are train locomotives that help steer large ships through the Panama Canal to prevent a ship from hitting and damaging the canal. The mules run on rack tracks, train tracks with a toothed rail down the middle to help the train climb steep inclines. The rack tracks run along both sides of the Panama Canal. Large ships are steered by four mules on each side of the ship, two in the front (bow) and two in the rear (stern). The mules are for steering and don't actually tow the ships. Smaller vessels don't use the mules, but instead use hand lines, which are controlled by the ship's crew.
Source: *the Virtual Panama website*

Crossing the Line

It was tradition in the Merchant Navy and indeed other navies, to hold a ceremony on board the ship to mark a sailor's first crossing of the equator. These rites of initiation have been notorious for their brutality; it was toned down on passenger carrying ships and used for passenger entertainment. Proceedings always involved King Neptune. Being forewarned by my friend Wayne about these procedures, I had built an alibi and for weeks had talked about a fictitious, port of call. I used Cape Town saying I had done a trip on a Union Castle Boat. I gleaned the information about the port from one of my many conversations with my friend Wayne who had visited the port.

As we got closer to the Equator I spelt out in graphic detail what had happened to me, to the wide-eyed first timers. I told them I had been tied to the mast and had my head shaved (in the sixties most young lads were proud of their locks as many tried to emulate the Beatles mop head craze). One young deckhand said, "*I don't care what you do to me but don't cut my hair*!" Probably the worse thing he could have said, as fellow shipmates could be quite cruel. This ruse spared me the crossing the line ceremony. I must admit I felt a little guilty as I helped search for the frightened quarry. We could not find one of the lads and the crew were starting to panic, as suggestions of a possible suicide like jumping overboard were bandied about.

After searching the ship three times, we eventually found him hiding in the forward rope locker covered with ropes and canvas. Unfortunately for him he was just putting off the inevitable.

We herded the three lads together, stripped them to their underwear and tied them to a mid-ships mast. Heads were roughly shaven, leaving clumps of hair in odd places. The Greasers added to the recipe by rubbing them down with dirty black oily rags to which they added a topping of sawdust. Next came the gathered buckets of ageing galley slops, including chickens entrails, which we liberally poured over their heads. With hands tied, they could not move. Being a hot humid day the ordeal did not bear thinking about. I felt sorry for these lads but at the same time kept thinking it could be worse, it could have been me!

One poor guy being initiated

Three hours later the sea hoses were set up and a high-pressure wash down removed all but the oil. Set free they made their way to the showers to try to scrub off the remaining oil. The ship's carpenter volunteered to be barber for the day and tidied the lads up as much as possible. Later that night after dinner, they were presented with 'Crossing the Line' certificates.

Our mop head friend quite liked his new look, said it made him look tougher and it was many months before he allowed his hair to grow again. This was a certificate I neither wanted nor attained, thanks to my inside knowledge. The secret stayed with me until payoff day. I am sure you can imagine the names they called me. Not to worry, I had crossed the line unscathed and luckily, for me, once you had crossed the line, you were free from any retrospective penalties.

Grass skirts and grey dust

Our next port of call was Nauru, also known as Ocean Island. It was the world's smallest island country, covering just 8.1 square miles, with a population second only to the Vatican City. The people were a friendly Polynesian race that had become rich because of the phosphate exports that were slowly eroding the island away. The official language was English, understood by almost all Nauruan's, although most of them still used Nauruan their native language. The main industries were fishing, coconuts and phosphate mining.

The Cape Wrath loading Phosphate in Nauru

The island is geographically oval; a single road serves to circumnavigate the perimeter, hugging the coast. The centre of the island was quite stark and ugly due to phosphate surface mining. This resulted in the loss of arable land; so much of the food had to be imported. The islanders suffered a high incidence of diabetes due to the consumption of processed foods.
Source: *Wikipedia encyclopaedia*

We lay offshore for two days while we waited for the cantilever loaders to become vacant. After berthing, within ten minutes, phosphate dust had completely covered the ship. It penetrated everywhere, even attacking the shelves of closed cupboards. The dust and acrid fumes drifted into the accommodation and invaded every nook and cranny. It contaminated the water supply and we had to run the taps before using the water for culinary purposes. Cleaning down the work surfaces every half hour became a real chore. Food had to be continually covered and protected. The late afternoon breeze only served to stir up more dust, before venturing out on deck we had to cover our mouths with handkerchiefs, but even they didn't stop the dust invading our throats. The thought that the dust consisted of centuries of bird droppings made gargling and mouth swilling a regular necessity. In the midday sun the cabins became unbearably hot, as blowers were turned off and portholes locked down. All outside doors had notices posted on them stating they must be closed after use. Working in the galley became unbearable, as the heat from the stoves added to the humidity. I had to change my working clothes almost on an hourly basis and resort to drinking large quantities of water, with salt tablets, to replenish what my body was losing by way of perspiration.

The dust blanket covered the few sad palm trees that graced the berth. The palms looked like a scene from a snowy Christmas card that served only to add to the bleakness.

It was a huge disappointment! I had been looking forward to seeing a beautiful South Pacific Island. I had imagined Polynesian girls in grass skirts dancing on the beach and greeting us with garlands of colourful exotic flowers to the strains of Hawaiian guitars. It is quite amazing what a few days at sea can do to the imagination. Instead, what did we get? About twenty Dockers covered in grey dust and a tickly throat and a cough that lasted for days.

Thankfully, with three cantilevers filling the hatches, we were fully loaded in ten hours and able to move out into the clear blue Pacific air. Three days later the deck crew were still hosing down the ship. The ship was gleaming as we entered Auckland harbour.

Chapter Six – New Zealand

Auckland

The rumour was that New Zealand was still suffering its loss of men from the war and the ratio of men to women was 40:60 although I think that estimate was wildly exaggerated.

However when the ship was alongside and tied up, a phone line was connected at the top of the gangway and it never stopped ringing. Female voices invited crewmembers to parties all over the city. After two days in Auckland, my mate on-board, a Liverpool lad called Don and I, accepted an invitation to a party hosted by nurses from The Auckland City Hospital.

Queen Street Auckland (photograph taken by author)

New Zealand didn't have bars and pubs, as we know them. They closed their doors at 6.30pm, so if you wanted a drink after that time, you bought a carry out and took it home. Even what little television there was terminated at 9pm. If you wanted a life after nine o'clock, you had to make your own fun. Friends would get together and organise a party, each contributing to the food, drink and venue. Parties would continue throughout most of the week, moving from house to house. Arrangements for the next party were usually made on the night, when all participants could plan together. All these parties created a great social scene and your circle of friends had the opportunity to expand after each new venue.

The older generation frowned on this party culture. The music, news and fashions of the sixties seemed to challenge the conservative values of 'the establishment'. Mods and Rockers were in abundance fuelled by influences from Britain and the rest of the outside world. Major protests relating to New Zealand sending troops to Vietnam were brewing across the land. This generation would rather make love than war.

I had arrived in New Zealand in a period of great change, which was rapidly dragging the country out of the stodgy 50's. To a visitor of this country, it appeared to be a country locked in the last decade, almost like watching a black and white movie, its people full of warmth and old-fashioned values.

Thank you, The Beatles!

Newspaper advertisement for The Beatles' concerts in Auckland on 24 and 25 June 1964

The Beatles New Zealand tour, 1964 21st June The Beatles arrive. 22nd and 23rd June Wellington concerts * 24 and 25 June Auckland concerts * 26 June Dunedin concert * 27 June Christchurch concert 28 June The Beatles leave.

On June 21st 1964, The Beatles landed at Wellington Airport to be greeted by 7000 screaming fans. The following eight days, until they flew out of Christchurch, hysteria reigned wherever they appeared. The occasion brought Auckland to a standstill and thousands of children bunked off school causing much concern to the local City Hall. More than just men's hairstyles changed after they went. Local music shops selling guitars did a roaring trade.

Don and I, having Liverpool accents drew the attention of most of the girls. A large group kept asking us to talk just to hear our accents and inquired if we knew Paul McCartney; of course we lied, I said Paul lived in a house not far from ours. Strangely I found out years later that Paul actually lived in a house on a road behind ours, although I never knew him. The local lads got rather irritated by all the attention we were getting. A lad from Birmingham tried to jump on the bandwagon telling a cluster of girls that he was from Liverpool in an unmistakably Birmingham accent. He was soon sent to the side lines along with the rest of the locals. We were having a great time and for probably the first time in my life, I had too much to drink.

It was late at night and some of the girls suggested that we go to their home in Panmure and continue partying. Alcohol was in full flow, as was the attention of the female of the species. We were having such a good time neither of us wanted to return to the ship and decided in the euphoria we would "*jump ship*".

The girls offered to let us stay in their house for as long as we wanted. Seven nurses shared a house. They said it was large enough for us all, plenty of room for two little scousers.

Jumping ship

With looming adventure on our minds, we took a taxi back to the Cape Wrath, to collect more beer and some of our belongings.

The Beatles arrive in Auckland

The excitement welled up and we were in a euphoric mood as we alighted the gangway. We were about to start a new chapter in life away from the hellhole that the Cape Wrath had become. Looking back, the party and drink played a huge part in the bravado we had suddenly attained. The third officer was on gangway duty. How would we get past him on the way back? We went to our cabins to pack the essentials, met up in the alleyway and stowed our bags out of sight. I then approached the Officer on duty and offered to watch the gangway while he went to the mess room to grab a coffee and sandwich. This worked a treat. When he was out of sight, Don and I grabbed our belongings and beer and beat a hasty retreat down the gangway.

The taxi driver went into a panic as he saw us descending the gangway, with suitcases and cases of beer. "*What are you doing?*" he shouted, "*You can't do that*" he said, "*I'll be in trouble if I let this happen*". We pleaded and cajoled him. Don flung the cases into the boot, mainly to get them out of view of any returning crew. After what seemed an age, both of us glancing back up the gangway, we managed to placate the driver with a large tip and a few beers.

At the dock gates the security guy walked out, hand raised and stopped the taxi, "*Right lads where are you off to in the early hours of the morning?*" We explained we had been to a party and were just getting some more beer. Don cheekily wrote down a false address and asked him to join us after he finished his shift, telling him the girls asked us to bring more men back. He said, "*Wish I could but don't get off till 8am besides, the spouse wouldn't approve!*" We laughed and joked with him, he eventually settled for six beers. He then let us through and told us to enjoy the party. As the docks disappeared behind us and to the considerable amusement of the driver, we both shouted, "*We're free!*" His amusement didn't last long. The driver complained he wasn't happy because he could have lost his licence. Then he burst into laughter and said, "*Wait till I tell my mates you even offered an invitation to the security guard to join you at the party. You Liverpool lads have some balls*". We left the taxi two roads away from the house. Friendly as he was, we decided we couldn't trust him enough not to give the game away.

We arrived back at the party and the fact that we had jumped ship made us the centre of attention even more and our celebrity lifestyle continued into the early hours of the morning.

"*Plenty of room*!" Ha! The two poor scousers had to share three mattresses pushed together with seven mad women...ah well! It was the permissive 60's.

What have we done?

The following afternoon three of the girls escorted us to the top of '*One Tree Hill*', so we could watch the Cape Wrath leave Auckland. It was such a beautiful day, lying back on the warm grass everything felt surreal. We lay there for almost two hours. I was suffering from a hangover, something totally alien to me. I kept glancing across to the distinctive yellow funnel, which was half hidden by downtown Auckland. We waited for signs of movement. Don said, "*They must be waiting for us to come back, no chance*!" I must admit I didn't have the bravado of Don as the enormity of our situation began to sink in.

Two blasts from the ships horn disturbed my worried thoughts; I looked up to see the ship leaving the harbour. "*Well, there is no going back now*", I thought. In quietness, we watched as the Cape Wrath moved out into the Bay. My eyes followed the ship until she disappeared behind Rangitoto Island. I suddenly remembered I had a camera with me, too late to get a picture of the ship leaving; I had to settle for the one shown on the next page.

I had feelings of guilt about the Third Officer on gangway duty. He would probably be in trouble for leaving his post. Don said, "*He hadn't seen us go ashore didn't know we had taken cases etc., so as far as he was concerned we'd just got tired of waiting and provided nobody saw the gangway unattended all would be none the wiser*." His reasoning made me feel a little better.

We were free... but in the cold light of day and at the back of my mind, the sudden realisation of what we had done hit me. I started thinking about the consequences of our actions. I thought of home. Would I ever get back? Coming from a close-knit family, I couldn't bear the thought of not seeing them again. In the sixties the world was so much larger than it is today it was harder to get from place to place. Here I was, a young lad of nineteen on the other side of the world. I thought of my family and my friends, Trixie the dog, at that moment I felt very alone and a little bit lost.

View from One Tree Hill, just after watching the ship leave Auckland

Back at the house I composed a letter home, trying to explain the reasons I was in this situation and asking mum and dad not to let the shipping company know my whereabouts. I had no doubt that they would have been in touch by now. After about twenty attempts I decided, the letter was fluent enough not to worry them unduly and with great trepidation, I posted it at the main post office on Queen Street. My return address was a box in the Main Post Office Auckland, I used this because the future was very uncertain as to where we would end up.

My thoughts were with my family all the time and I wrote home and sent cards as often as possible to keep them from worrying about me.

Don and I decided that we needed new identities, in case the police stopped us at any time. I decided to call myself Robert Yates. My mate at home was called Wayne Yeats, so although spelled differently, it was easy to remember. I cannot remember what Don called himself. Every morning we would buy The Auckland Herald newspaper, look up what ship was in port and adopt that ship as an alibi. For instance, one day I may be Robert Yates second cook off the Auckland Star, another day a City boat would be our alibi. Fortunately, the police never stopped us, as the port was a bustling, thriving port, swamped with many nationalities, which changed as each day passed.

Chapter Seven – A New Beginning

Finding work

Between us, we had little money and knew that we had to find work very quickly. The girls offered to support us, but that was totally out of the question. We scoured the local newspapers, and walked from door to door. Work seemed to be plentiful, so we were able to be selective.

In two days, with very little effort I had found a job with a company called "*Refrigerated Appliances*" They were based in Dominion Road, Mount Eden. Nobody asked for papers in those days. I said I'd been working in Christchurch South Island for six months, keeping details as vague as possible in case I slipped up. I was offered a position there and then with a next day start.

Refrigerated Appliances (photo taken by the author)

I was to become second man to Pete, a refrigeration engineer. Pete was in his thirties with a rugged face and a really dry sense of humour. From the first day we got on really well and although he had great difficulty understanding my Liverpool accent, I soon had him talking in my native tongue and confusing all around him back at the unit, so much so, that some of the girls named him Ringo. We became known as the Paul and Ringo team. One morning we arrived at the unit to be greeted by a Paul and Ringo sticker adorning the windscreen of the company van. Put there by a couple of girls in the office. We'd often return to the unit singing the latest Beatles hits that I taught him while driving to various jobs. What other job could you go out singing in the morning and return singing at night. I declared him an honorary scouser and he took great pride in using his newfound accent as a party piece, often fooling fellow New Zealanders for most of the evening. I'd play along with him to add to the fun; occasionally he'd slip back into his native accent, which would give the game away.

I was also to help back at the unit when not on the road. Phil, the owner, was quite a reserved and kindly man. He took me under his wing and treated me like a son from the beginning. The work environment made it a joy to go to work. In fact it didn't feel like work, it was an adventure and every day was different, every job different, with new things to learn. One day I may be out on the road helping to install giant fridges in a supermarket, the next I would be fixing or re-gassing fridge units in people's homes or retail units. Yes, happy days all overseen by Phil who ran the company like a beautifully oiled clock. He treated everyone as family; was very much respected and was rewarded by happy staff that really worked hard for him. His motto was, "*we should all work to live and enjoy life, not live to work*"

Don was a real ladies' man, slim with jet-black hair and piercing blue eyes. He was always at the front of the queue in attracting members of the opposite sex. He tried out three or four jobs in as many weeks. The first job, was in a chocolate factory, where he would return after work bloated and sick from eating too much of the produce. When it started affecting his nightlife, he said, "*Enough is enough, I'm gonna end up fat and slovenly*". He eventually settled down in a shoe factory. He said, "*The pay isn't up to much but, being surrounded by women more than compensated*". One thing that made us stand out from the crowd was our style of dress. At that time New Zealand's fashion seemed to be ten years behind the UK. Wherever we went, people would quiz us about our clothing, although comments were mainly complimentary, we started to feel like aliens. Our first pay cheque was squandered on local clothes and even though we felt awkward in them, it helped us blend into the background. After a couple of weeks we reverted to our own clothes, as it became clear, that there was always a large percentage of Brits in port, due to the flourishing trade with New Zealand. Most of the fears formed in our own minds. Don had only lasted a couple of days in local clothes, before he reverted back, his excuse "*the women have stopped talking to me*" laughable I know, it was all in his mind, as he was never short of female company.

Setup

Pete and I were called out to repair a fridge in Ponsonby, a squalid part of town with large terraced houses that had seen better days. The address stood out as very impressive, clean and its exterior paintwork lit up the otherwise drab surroundings. Pete sat in the van and said, "*I need to do some paperwork and organise the next job*". He told me, "*It's a simple, re-gassing job; you are well qualified to do it on your own*". I grabbed the toolbox and gas bottle and made my way to the imposing entrance.

A large buxom, scantily dressed lady opened the door. I immediately became aware that the interior surroundings were in sharp contrast to the exterior. The walls were painted dark red and black gossamer fabric draped every window and doorway. Incense filled the air; my mind went into overdrive, as I tried to make sense of my surroundings. She showed me into a large kitchen, filled with black sofas and giant red cushions. The huge fridge in the corner of the room required a great deal of effort, as I struggled to move it. On opening the fridge door I noticed it was full of wine and beers of all kinds. The local beer was DB Bitter. (Dominion Breweries), or Lion beer, but this fridge was full of beers of the world. I recognised Tennant's and Watney's Red Barrel from back home, filling me with warm nostalgia as I realised that this was more of a party room than kitchen.

The scantily dressed lady, showing no embarrassment whatsoever, offered me some New Zealand draft. She deftly poured it before I had chance to decline. I had work to do, so I set to work on a huge drinks fridge. I sensed movement behind me and became aware of eyes watching me, I turned to find the room filled with ladies in various states of undress, edging closer, running their fingers through my hair, trying to tease me, massaging my shoulders and plying me with drinks etc. They kept moving my tools and then asking me to come and find them, after having secreted them away in various parts of their underwear. A spanner went missing, after many minutes looking for it, a pair of large negligee encased breasts appeared over my shoulder inviting me to retrieve it! What should have been a ten-minute job turned into 45 minutes. I felt so embarrassed, I just wanted to finish the job and go, besides I had taken far too long doing the job, I wondered why Pete hadn't been to investigate. I returned red faced to the van Pete said, "*What took you so long? We are going to be late for the next job!*"

Before I could reply, the look on my face had him bursting into uncontrollable laughter. He explained to me in between fits of laughter "*The address was a house of ill-repute and a very good refrigeration customer*", he hastened to add! Phil and Pete had planned and conspired with Madam Flora Mckenzie the whole setup. Well, it certainly worked, Flora reported to Phil, that I was very professional and a gentleman throughout, they couldn't do anything to stop me doing my job; and yes, the fridge was working perfectly! If the truth was known I wasn't professional I was just terrified!

Everyone back at the unit teased me for weeks. If I was ever late for work, they would ask, "*Where have you been, Flora Mackenzie's?*" or sometimes "*Flora called and said, can you send that nice engineer again?*" they all certainly made hay out of that episode.

Everything was all in good humour and it really was a great workplace and a fun place to turn up everyday. Everyone got on, no backstabbing, or ill feeling, we all worked as a team.

Flora MacKenzie (or McKenzie) was born in Mangere, Auckland, on 15 August 1902, the daughter of Hugh Ross MacKenzie, a farmer and his wife, Lillie Theresa Ellett. Flora, her brother and sister were brought up on the horse farm their parents owned, which became well known as the Ascot stud. McKenzie Road in Mangere was named after her father, who was an active member of both the Mangere Road Board and the Auckland Racing Club. Later Sir Hugh, he went on to achieve prominence as long-time chairman of the Auckland Harbour Board. In February 1927 her father officially welcomed the duke and duchess of York when they arrived at Auckland.

Flora MacKenzie trained as a nurse and also became an accomplished dressmaker. For many years she ran a boutique, Ninette, in Vulcan Lane, which specialised in bridal gowns and was reputedly patronised by an affluent clientele, which included cabinet ministers' wives. She sketched her own creations, often in watercolours. (After her death, framed dress sketches by Flora MacKenzie were sold in an Auckland gallery, often, it was claimed, to former clients of her other business venture -- the infamous Ring Terrace brothel in Ponsonby).

MacKenzie's entry into the world of prostitution has been traced back to the 1940s, when her father purchased a block of flats for her at 17–19 Ring Terrace. Flora MacKenzie apparently lived there for six months before realising that the tenants were 'good-time girls' who entertained American GIs.

She is then said to have drifted into the role of madam when her frequent drinking binges allowed the 'professional' girls to take over the premises. The establishment developed and was like an exclusive club that attracted patronage from Auckland's business and commercial élite.

It also attracted the attention of the police. Between 1962 and 1976 Flora MacKenzie appeared in court six times on brothel-keeping charges and was twice imprisoned for periods of six months. One of these appearances was sparked by reaction to threats made by NZ Truth newspaper in 1968 to publish the names of the owners of cars seen parked outside the Ring Terrace establishment. The police responded to complaints and used undercover officers to obtain evidence of brothel keeping. Kevin Ryan defended MacKenzie at the resultant trial, during which the judge, G. D. Speight and the jury were taken to her property to ascertain for themselves whether this was a brothel or, as MacKenzie said, simply a large house let as flats and used for entertaining. Ryan recalled his astonishment at the transformation the premises had undergone before the judicial visit. A large cross, dominated the notice board in the lounge, where pamphlets proclaimed 'Jesus Saves' and invited people to attend a Billy Graham crusade. As the jury walked through the flats they were somewhat confused to see only single beds, on top of which lay large, ornate Bibles. Some were persuaded by Ryan's argument that Flora MacKenzie was a lonely woman who liked company and gave young women a good roof over their heads and the trial resulted in a hung jury.

Flora MacKenzie had by now become an Auckland identity. Her home was legendary, prized for its art and antiques and rumoured to have a rotating bed upstairs with panoramic harbour views. She has been described as 'a flamboyant, happy-go-lucky woman who did not care a damn about what the so-called respectable people thought of her'. She was an alcoholic who sought help from Alcoholics Anonymous, somewhat unsuccessfully. She pretended she liked drinking milk and bought two pints a day, which she then mixed liberally with spirits and kept in the refrigerator. Whenever anyone from AA visited, MacKenzie beamed virtuously as she sipped her 'milk'.

Flora MacKenzie was also a great lover of animals, in particular her Pekinese dogs. When, in 1957, she discovered that one of her pets had been run over, she immediately blamed a neighbour. This woman, a justice of the peace, answered a loud knock on her door, only to have a flying dead dog hurtle into her: MacKenzie had swung the animal round by its tail until the door opened, when she suddenly let go. The neighbour phoned the police and Alec Leyland was sent to attend the incident. This was the occasion of the first of many meetings with Flora MacKenzie, which became more numerous a year or so later when he joined the Vice Squad. Although adversaries, they became firm friends.

The Ring Terrace brothel became the most famous in Auckland, if not New Zealand. MacKenzie, however, never liked the words 'brothel' or 'prostitute,' and contended, 'Isn't every woman a prostitute? Married men pay their wives, don't they?' She preferred to describe her business as offering 'sex therapy,' and indeed sexologists are said to have referred clients to her for remedial assistance. Flora MacKenzie believed in equal rights for women and declared, 'I think men are useless b—s, running around crying because they need sex. But I'm not a man hater, what's good for one should be good for the other and I think the time will come when there are places for women to go for men. I think women should be able to choose the men, buy one and then drop him afterward like they drop women'.

At the time of her death, at her home on 8 July 1982, she had cirrhosis of the liver and a weak heart. She had been ill and in pain for some years. Flora MacKenzie had never married nor borne children and was rumoured to have left her premises to the man who delivered her weekly crate of whisky; all her money went to the deaf. Although no death notice was published and her funeral was a very quiet affair, the obituaries and tributes to her were fond and numerous. Amongst those who paid tribute to MacKenzie was one of her former legal counsel, Roger Maclaren, who said; 'She was generous to a fault and always a sucker for a soft touch. She had an amazing sense of humour, she was garrulous, obscene -- she was everything a madam should be, I suppose'.

Source: Jan Jordan. 'MacKenzie, Flora - Biography,' from the Dictionary of New Zealand Biography. Te Ara - the Encyclopaedia of New Zealand, updated 1-Sep-10

URL: http://www.TeAra.govt.nz/en/biographies/5m19/1

Happy days

On days spent back at the unit, rather than stand around, I would take it upon myself to do a spot of painting or cleaning, anything to keep me busy. Phil said he had never seen the unit look so good. My work ethos from the Merchant Navy served me well, besides, the days passed more quickly. New Zealand in the sixties was all about leisure time and partying!

Pete, the Engineer, had really taken to the Beatles and the whole Mersey sound. He used to quiz me about Liverpool and the various Liverpool groups. On our way to a job in Hamilton we would sing a selection of the latest Beatles hits. I use the word 'sing' in the loosest of terms. He would try to imitate my Liverpool accent. All the way to Hamilton, out of tune renditions of "*Can't buy me love*" or "*Penny Lane*" would escape the confines of the car to the displeasure of all in earshot. One particularly hot day with windows down, we came to halt at a road junction. An elderly couple pulled up alongside us, stared and then suddenly burst into song joining us with "*It's been a hard day's night*". We laughed all the way to Hamilton. They looked so prim and proper, almost as if they had just come from a Bible class; it was so unexpected.

Rugby was Pete's favourite topic and the famous All Blacks were never far from conversation. I tried to convert him to football. I was so proud that Bill Shankly had just taken Liverpool FC to top of the Football league. I told him to be a real scouser he'd have to become a football fan. Ed would have none of it, he taught me a Parody set to the tune of "*My Old Mans A Dustman*" It went as follows:

Oh, my old man's an All Black,
He wears the silver fern,
But his mates just couldn't take him So he's out now for a turn.
Da-dit-dit-da da-dit-dit-da da-dit-dit-da-da-da
Well, dad's played rugby all his life
And it's very plain to see
He's trying very hard
To make an All Black out of me:
"Son don't you worry if you get punched
When your down in a scrum,
Just you wait 'til there's a ruck
And you can fix the guilty one!
Oh, my old man's an All Black,
He wears the silver fern,
But his mates just couldn't take him
So he's out now for a turn.
Da-dit-dit-da da-dit-dit-da da-dit-dit-da-da-da
So he's out---- now----- for a turn------ !
Der ditdit Da, Der ditdit Da, Dee ditdit Da da Da
So he's out-- now-- for-- a-- turn!

It wasn't long before we reverted back to the Mersey sound; rugby wasn't my scene at all. Yes, life was good, the work was varied and carefree and evenings were fun filled and exciting! Time went on and I really settled into the job. I enjoyed the varied routines.

Every day was different; I was working with a friendly like-minded team and learning new skills. It was such a close knit family firm and when things were quiet, Phil would pack us into a truck and whisk us off to the ninety mile beach where we could swim, I attempted to surf, but could never get the hang of it! When the season was in we would dig for Toheroas, a shellfish delicacy endemic to the shores of New Zealand, often made into soup, for which it has an international reputation. They were like huge Mussels, measuring up to seven or eight inches long. It was a learning

111

curve digging for Toheroas. During my early attempts we were taught to look for small holes and bubbles in the wet sand, in my haste I almost sliced the top of one of my fingers off. They have an almost blade like shell. Needless to say, it didn't happen again as I took to digging with a spade like clamshell, until the delicacy was exposed. I managed to catch what they said was the largest one they had seen. "*What a beaut*" they cried, as everyone milled around to get a closer look.

Phil took command, organised the food and lit and manned the barbecue. Toheroas made a wonderful soup and this would be followed by all manner of grilled meats. Phil's friend was a butcher so we always had the best prime cuts and we were always left with a surplus of food. Then Phil would invite others on the beach to join us and we'd party until the sun went down. Yes, life was blissful at work and play.

Phil's car disaster

For months, Phil had been awaiting delivery of a brand new Holden EH Station Wagon. A new car was a rarity as the only way you could bring a new car into the country was to have money outside of New Zealand. He had opened an

Holden EH Station Wagon – similar to the one Phil owned

account in Australia for that purpose. The existing cars on the road therefore had to be looked after, hence the reason there were so many older cars in good condition out and about.

The day he picked it up, he asked me to go with him and then he planned to take me on to a large job in Rotorua to join some lads already in place. Rotorua was roughly 140 miles away. Phil was proudly showing off his new car and familiarising himself with the controls, when we nearly came to an untimely end; ascending a steep gradient in front of us was a large chemical tanker. It seemed to have three large domes across the top of the tank. As Phil was talking, I noticed the back dome starting to waver, I called out to warn Phil, who immediately applied his brakes to try to put some distance between us and the tanker, at the same time he was hitting his horn to warn the other driver. A gust of wind caught the dome and sent it hurtling onto the highway and like a giant wheel. It started to meander all over the road towards us. Phil fought with the car to evade a collision, swerving left and right. Fortunately, the dome missed us and rolled harmlessly into some trees at the side of the highway. We gave chase to inform the tanker driver, who was unaware of what had happened,

We progressed onto Rotorua and a few miles up the road ran into a traffic jam, an unusual occurrence in those days, as traffic was quite sparse. After about twenty minutes, we assumed there must have been an accident ahead. Drivers started showing signs of frustration. Ahead some vehicles started turning to head back the way they had come. Stuck in front of us was a large farm truck; steam seemed to be coming from the back and by the smell we surmised it was carrying manure. It was a hot day and we had to close the windows as the smell was overpowering. In those days there was no air-conditioning and soon we were both drenched with sweat, sitting in wet shirts. The driver of the farm vehicle decided to reverse and make what would possibly be a five-point turn. As he reversed we could see he was going to back into us,

Phil once again pressed his horn, but to no avail. With a grinding crunching crash, the back end of the truck rode backwards over our bonnet, forcing both of us to make a hasty retreat out of Phil's newly acquired pride and joy.

I felt so sorry for Phil, he had waited eight months for his car only to have it wrecked before it had covered a hundred miles or so. He even joked, "*A brand new car and the horn's worn out already!*" Once again, Phil showed his calm nature, not a hint of anger, he then stated, "*It's only a car at least we didn't get injured*". I was choked for him, but couldn't help but smile. What a great attitude to life. A couple of hours later the traffic cleared and a tow truck arrived to move the car and us to Rotorua. Because it was a brand new model, it took months to get parts to affect a repair.

The bee's knees

Not to be outdone, Don and I pooled our resources and bought an old Austin 7. It was vintage 1937 black and an absolute rust bucket, but it was all we could afford. Because of its poor condition, we managed to negotiate a much better price. We collected it and Don took the wheel. I hung on to the passenger door that had fallen off after about half a mile. All the way home,

The Austin 7 - similar to but in much better condition than our rust bucket

I was wrestling the door at every bump and turn. The leather door strap and window frame took the strain as the door fought with me to leave the car again. No such things as seat belts then, so I had to fight to stay in the car.

Don was in a mischievous mood and did his best to negotiate over as many potholes as possible, his laughter almost drowning out my protestations. Sometimes his mad ways took over his sensible head. We had just spent most of our earnings to acquire transport; he almost wrecked it within the first ten minutes. Back at the house, we managed to secure the car door with rope and wire, which limited our access to one side only. *"Not conducive to pulling the Sheila's"* Don remarked! The door hinges and straps were so deteriorated; we could not afford to get them fixed, so it was a scramble to manoeuvre across the drivers seat, for all but the driver. I must say the Sheila's were not impressed with our mode of transport, but once we managed to squeeze them in, it became a laughter wagon. We would make our way to one of the many secluded beautiful beaches; the girls brought along the picnic, we supplied the beer. Some of the beaches were so remote, with no transport for miles. It was fingers crossed that the old Austin would start and get us home again.

As wrecked as the car was we thought we were the bee's knees. We were mobile and had our own transport! Although, everywhere we travelled, belching black smoke followed us. The engine soon packed in, it went with a bang and the car clattered to a halt about three miles from home. Our friendly neighbour towed it back to the house. He was a mechanic and managed to get it running again, but said, *"If I was you I'd get rid before you kill yourself"*. It lasted another three days before the engine finally packed in. We abandoned it on a side street in Mount Roskhill, a suburb in Auckland. Our heady days of car ownership came to a sudden and heart-breaking end. So it was back to the buses and shank's pony for us.

A small world

It was a hot summers day and I was strolling down Queen Street, which was the main shopping street in Auckland, minding my own business; window shopping and enjoying a day off, when a scouse accent hailed me from behind *"Alright… I know you, you're from Speke, seen you with your big ally"* (Alsatian). I turned around but didn't recognise him at all. It seems he knew me by sight, walking Trixie, back home in Speke. He had just docked in Auckland on a City Boat. What a chance meeting on the other side of the world!

We spent the afternoon in Ma Gleason's*, a seaman's pub near the harbour reminiscing about back home. He invited me back on board for a meal, but I couldn't take a chance, fearing that going into the docks again would leave me open to being caught. I met him again in the Seaman's Mission in Amsterdam two years later. I was in the cinema watching a film, *"The Great Escape"*. At the intermission, the lights came on and that familiar voice rang out *"Alright"*. I find it

Queen Street Auckland

quite amazing that our paths crossed twice in two different places half way around the world, but to this day, I have never met or seen him in Liverpool.

Letters would arrive from home. Mum would write and I would receive letters from Bob and Eileen Roberts who were and still are to this day, close friends of the family. After reading the letters I would feel even more homesick, Don and I would go to Ma Gleason's just to mix with some of the recently arrived seamen from Liverpool and to ingest any news from our beloved hometown.

*Ma Gleason's had a way of circumnavigating the law to enable the seamen to continue drinking into the early hours of the morning. They would sell tickets for a nominal fee, confirming you were booked into a room. This enabled you to drink well after the 6pm closing time. I don't know how they got away with it as the number of rooms were very few and sometimes up to forty seamen had supposedly booked rooms! However most times we would buy a carry out and accept an invitation to one of the many parties, I was never a drinker and preferred the party scene rather than spend my time with drunken sailors.

Time to jump ship again

Meanwhile, back at the 'nurses home' life was getting very uncomfortable for Don and me. Our respective girl friends wanted a more serious relationship. This didn't fit in with our plans, we were far too young and both of us wanted to eventually make our way home. Bitchiness and jealousy raged. Arguments over nothing flared, an innocent comment, or a glance across the room and the girls would accuse us of flirting with other women. This started to make life miserable. Amidst the fun and laughter, there were undercurrents of angry words and unpleasant confrontations. We started to feel the rumblings of possessiveness and control and we both decided enough was enough. We needed a way out. We decided it was time for us to 'jump ship' again.

We scoured The New Zealand Herald and The Auckland Star newspapers, looked in various property shop windows and eventually found a lovely wooden detached property to rent in an up and coming resort on the edge of Auckland. It was ranch style with a veranda to the front of the property. At the bottom of the garden, over a wall made of planks and driftwood we had our own private beach. Prior to work in the mornings we often went for a swim. On balmy evenings, it was a great place to hold parties and for very little rent, we had our own bit of paradise.

After three weeks, two Australian girls moved in with us, insisting in taking a share in the finances. Helen was a petite very attractive girl, with eyes that sparkled happiness. She worked as a receptionist in an optician's shop. She was always smartly turned out and a few years older than me. She had a very bubbly nature, full of life and surprises. We partied four nights a week; life was hectic but great fun.

Don's girl Evelyn, was a very pretty brunette but with a moody disposition and prone to bouts of depression. She often had thoughts of her hometown Sydney and a broken relationship she had left behind. At times, it took all we could muster to cheer her up, but on the good days she joined in the fun, on bad days she was a very different person, with an almost a Jeckyl and Hyde quality. Don, a real ladies man, was finding her hard to deal with, after a short time the inevitable happened. Evelyn made her way back to Sydney and probably the arms of the man she had left behind. Don did not seem too concerned and within three weeks one of his female colleagues from work Pat, had moved in.

Television was new to Auckland and only introduced in 1960. To own one increased your circle of friends. Our mechanic neighbour Bill invited us in every Sunday evening to watch The BBC World News programme. We would get pride of place on the thirties style deep red moquette sofa, watching the little box as he called it, although I don't know why he called it a little box as the cabinet was huge in relation to the tiny screen. We eagerly anticipated Sunday evenings; it was our only real contact with what was happening back at home.

Any news of home brought tingles of sadness when thinking of what we had left behind.

I remember programmes like *Larry the Lamb*, *Dragnet*, *The Twilight Zone*, *I love Lucy*, and *Dangerman*. We spent many beer-filled hours watching the teak encased black and white flickering television. Bill spent most of the time on the roof, fiddling with the aerial trying to maximise the reception. As a consequence, he had a permanent ladder attached to the guttering. We always seemed to lose the picture when anything of interest appeared. In retrospect this was early days of television, so to get a picture at all created excitement, how things have changed, in my short lifetime.

Chapter Eight – Tough Times

Arrested

Life had a real cosy feeling about it, Helen and I were getting on really well and I was warming to her infectious sense of humour. She never displayed a care in the world, her bubbly personality shone wherever we went. There was nothing really serious about the relationship; we just lived for the moment. All our friends thought we made a perfect couple, but we both thought we were far too young for anything serious, we just revelled in each other's company.

One balmy evening we strolled down to the waterfront and treated ourselves to a burger and a glass of wine. A light fresh breeze cooled the warm evening air. The port was bustling and the waters sparkled. Small craft and sailing boats wended their way past cargo ships at anchor. Fishing boats, followed by swarms of hungry noisy seagulls, made their way home after a hard day's work. We became so engrossed in all the activity; we almost missed the beginning of the movie. Running up Queen St, we managed to enter the cinema just as The Pink Panther's title screen played. What an enjoyable film. We laughed all the way through; a great movie. Leaving the cinema, we jostled hand in hand through the happy departing crowds. We didn't seem to have a care in the world as we chatted and laughed about some of the scenes in the film.

Circumstances suddenly changed. I was roughly seized from behind, an authoritative voice spat in my ear, "T*ensing Ng I'm arresting you for illegally extending your stay in New Zealand*". The voice belonged to one of three plain clothed officers. I protested my innocence and tried to bluff my way out of it using the name Robert Yates, but that didn't work as they produced a copy of my discharge book photo. My mind was racing as all kinds of thoughts went through my head. Would I be thrown into jail? Would there be a court case? I wondered what the penalty was for being an illegal immigrant? How would I be returned to England? I was thinking of all my friends, things half said, half finished. Would I be allowed to say goodbye? What would Phil say? After all the trust he had put in me. I felt I had deceived my work colleagues. What would they think? I had managed to keep my cards close to my chest and as far as I was aware, nothing had slipped out.

They had pulled Helen away from me, she stood about ten yards away, talking to a police officer and sobbing, she was well aware of my situation in New Zealand. My heart went out to her, minutes before we were in the happiest of moods, not a care in the world, in a flash our world was turned upside down. It felt as if the skies had darkened and grown heavy and our little world had collapsed around us. I asked if I could talk to Helen, but was refused. "*Just say goodbye*" the uncaring officer said, I shouted across "*Don't worry Helen, I'll be in touch*". As I spoke they, pushed me up against the wall and clamped handcuffs on me. They escorted Helen in the opposite direction along Queen Street and out of sight. Within ten minutes, a police car arrived and I was whisked away to an office near the docks for further questioning. They asked me if I knew the whereabouts of Don, I lied and told them I didn't realise Don had jumped ship. Hoping all the time Helen would alert him to my predicament.

Later that night I was moved to Mt Eden Gaol. I was told I would stay there overnight until they received my documents from the ship's last port of call in New Zealand before deciding what to do with me. As I entered the miserable grey castle like building, my heart sank, I asked myself "*Would this be my home for the next few months?*" I later found out that one of the nurses from the house in Panmure, who had seen us in the cinema had grassed me... Ah well poetic justice I suppose.

Once inside the Jail, I was searched and my personal effects were taken from me, including shoelaces and tie. They placed them in a large brown envelope that was sealed and signed by two officers, who I felt, were doing their best to unsettle me. *"What trade do want to learn lad? We have them all in here; murderers, rapists, bank robbers... tell us and we'll fix you up with a tutor"* I jokingly said, *"jail breaker"*. My Liverpool sense of humour didn't work, as I was rewarded with a resounding slap to the back of the head that sent me spinning across the room. They then reiterated I was to be kept in overnight to await my documents from Christchurch, the Cape Wrath's last port of call in New Zealand.

Looking back, I am sure they were trying to scare me, what were they doing housing me in a high security prison and not a local police cell, for the misdemeanour of jumping ship. Jumping ship was so prevalent in the sixties, as New Zealand was such a beautiful country and work was plentiful. I was told that the next day I was to meet the officials who would

Mt. Eden Gaol

organise my departure from New Zealand. I was escorted to a small dingy damp cell with a single bed, graffiti and not much else. I was thankful that none of my prospective tutors were occupants; at least I had a cell to myself, but how long will this last?

I tried to sleep, but my mind was alive and buzzing, I could not help but worry about Helen and Don, I tossed and turned and eventually I must have dozed off. In the early hours of the morning I awoke, startled, with loud shouts and bangs pounding in my head, "*Where was I?*" my brain took moments for everything to click into place. The racket seemed to come from a distance, was I dreaming? Someone, I assumed it was a warder, swung open the door. "*Get out, the place is in flames,*" he cried, with that, he quickly moved on to the next cell. Men gathered out in the walkway. Prisoners were rushing up and down and shouting, dancing, some as if in celebration, It was determined that a riot had started in an adjoining block. Some of the men decided to join in "*Come on! Drag out your bedding; we're setting this place alight*" Prisoners were throwing anything they could into the centre of the block, beds, chairs, furniture, personal effects, anything that could be lifted and smashed down from the upper level, it was absolute mayhem. I felt I was in a nightmare; shocked and dazed, my heart thumping, I stayed where I was. The men carried on to the next cell swearing and shouting almost manic. I had no intention of getting involved, I was only there for the night. I sat in the comparative safety of my cell, while all hell broke loose outside. After a short time the acrid smell of smoke became overbearing, my eyes were stinging; I started spluttering and coughing. It was time to leave. I clambered over the wreckage, as I endeavoured to find a safer place.

I joined some men who also wanted no part, bonded and kept moving away from the trouble. A few skirmishes happened with the troublemakers and fights broke out. The hours dragged on, but time seemed to stand still, as I wished for it all to end. Soon the rioters were drawn away to throw anything they could at the fire fighters on the outside, who were trying to douse the flames. All around, the rumours spread. In the background someone shouted, "*They've brought in the army!*" Then we heard that the ringleaders had surrendered, but still sporadic fighting ensued and the frenzied voices of men shouting fed an already hostile atmosphere. I attributed the odd sharp crack to gunfire. Next, a group of prisoners ran past the cell that I was sitting in, chased by riot police with batons and shields. The sight of us stopped the police in their tracks, a team of around eight with riot shields and batons moved toward the four of us. We had been sitting passively against a wall, but they set about us flailing their batons at any part of the body they could hit, I tried to protect myself, but my arms and legs then became targets. I was hit seven or eight times and was bruised and sore for weeks after. They dragged and shoved us to the perimeter walls. The prison looked like a scene from a war movie still smouldering and awash with dirty water. Eventually police rounded all the inmates up and we were moved to vans just outside the perimeter walls. After about an hour they moved us to a holding room to wait questioning.

The disturbance followed a botched escape attempt and lasted into the next day. Several warders were taken hostage and part of the prison was gutted by fire.

Mt Eden Prison is one of New Zealand's oldest prisons. An imposing, castle-like structure of basalt rock, its design was based on English models and a belief that life in prison should be unpleasant.

By the 1960s, prison life had moved on from the floggings and dark cells of the previous century. But at Mt Eden maximum-security prisoners still languished in solitary confinement with no access to hobbies or recreation. Recent clamp-downs on conditions, along with problems of overcrowding, may have contributed to the riot.

At 2 a.m. on 20 July, two prisoners making a break for it clubbed the unlucky warder who discovered them, took two hostages and set about unlocking cells. Chaos ensued as the newly liberated inmates' lit fires and fuelled them with oil, furniture and their own personal effects. Firemen had to retreat under a barrage of bricks and other missiles.

Armed police, warders and troops stood guard around the prison and used warning shots and high-powered hoses to discourage break-outs. Eventually the lack of food, fuel and shelter took its toll and the prisoners surrendered 33 hours after the riot began. The rebellious mood spread: conflicts broke out and fires were started at Wellington's Mt Crawford Prison and Paparua Prison in Christchurch.

The damage at Mt Eden was extensive. Basements, storerooms, the kitchen, chapel, watch house and 61 cells were destroyed and the prison roof was extensively damaged. The riot was followed by further calls for the prison to be demolished. Prisoners were relocated while the gutted shell was rebuilt.

Today, Mt Eden is a medium-security facility for up to 521 male inmates. In June 2007 the Department of Corrections announced plans to build a modern prison at the site and convert the old building into administrative space. Heritage features will be retained, but the barbed wire has had its day. It was announced in 2010 that the new prison will be privately run, as was the old one between2000 and 2005.

Source: http://www.nzhistory.net.nz/mt-eden-jail-riot, (Ministry for Culture and Heritage), updated 12-Aug-2011

Battered and bruised

I was tired bruised and dirty. Blood was running down my chin, the taste of fresh blood filled my mouth and I was half sitting half lying on the floor.

After being questioned about who I was, I had answered truthfully stating that I was only being detained overnight and the suit I was wearing belonged to me. Next a shout of "*LIAR!*", followed quickly by a blow to the mouth, knocking me cleanly off the chair. The unexpected fall to the floor didn't give me time to react. A sickening crunch was felt to the back of my head as it hit the wooden panelling on the wall, the effect of which seemed to reverberate through my whole body. Dazed and shocked I looked up at the large overweight; ginger haired official standing over me. His fists were clenched and his face was getting redder by the second. He then again accused me of stealing a warder's suit to try to escape.

I prepared to defend myself from the next onslaught. The other official remonstrated with him and told him to calm down and taking him by the arm he pulled him away from me. They shouted at each other almost coming to blows, he backed off and said to his colleague "*I need a break*". I was glad to see him leave the room.

Mt. Eden ablaze during the riots

About ten minutes later a plain clothed official replaced him; he came armed with some tea and biscuits. It was the first food and drink I'd had since the riots had begun. He took a much softer and easy-going approach. He asked me about my home in England and said he had some relations in Manchester. He seemed to be going out of his way to make up for his colleague's aggressive behaviour, but right through the interview I was on the edge of my seat waiting for something to explode again. It seemed that many records and documents had been burnt during the riots making it very difficult to identify anybody. When again questioned about the suit I was wearing, I removed the jacket and pointed to the inside label J. Hepworth & Sons, a retail shop from back home. I also discovered attached to the inside pocket a little pink dry cleaning ticket, with a number and underneath in small print 'South Liverpool'. From then on, it was plain sailing; the questions softened and I noticed a more concerned attitude. A few more questions and they realised I was telling the truth. Looking back the police officer must have been as fatigued as I was; they were working all hours through the riots.

The machine gun killer

Mt. Eden remains after the riots

Everything was in complete chaos and the officials were unable to check if my papers had arrived from South Island. I had to spend another night in jail. They told me it was going to be a bit crowded, owing to the influx of Mount Eden inmates. At least I was going to stay in Auckland, unlike some prisoners who would be shipped all over North Island. They gave me some sandwiches and a mug of tea. I was then allowed to clean myself up and I started to feel human again. In a matter of hours I was transported in a van, along with ten or twelve other prisoners to a local Auckland police station. I was to be housed overnight in one of its four cells. I still had no shoelaces, and my personal belongings were probably still smouldering in the ruins. After such a long time, all I wanted was a good bath, but that wasn't going to happen soon.

On arrival, they gave me a dirty old grey army blanket; it had a musty smell and was threadbare down one side. I stood waiting in line and was then escorted to one of the four small cells in a square courtyard, and told to make myself comfortable. The door opened to a nauseating smell of sick and vomit, all around the floor and walls laid the bodies of men trying to get some form of sleep. The cell measured about ten feet square and was already very overcrowded. One guy was retching in the corner, another was bloodied, moaning in pain and holding a blood soaked bandage to the side of his face. There was hardly room to sit never mind lie down but overcome with tiredness I eventually found myself a spot half lying, half sitting against a wall. I couldn't sleep, not with the large guy next to me snoring so loudly. His snoring became a major irritation; I angrily nudged him with my foot shouting at him to shut up! He opened his eyes, gave me an evil glare, pulled the blanket over himself and turned his body away. The night dragged on, finding it very hard to keep my eyes closed, I eventually dozed off.

Early next morning we were awakened by the sound of the cell door opening, we were all moved into the centre courtyard to use one of the two toilets available.

I struck up a conversation with a guy that was in a similar situation to me; he was only in overnight for a fracas at his home where he had tried to eject some unwanted gatecrashers. As we were talking, he pointed out the guy who had been the attention of my nudging foot "*You know who that is don't you*?" I shook my head. "*That's Gillies the Machine gun Killer*". I thought silently to myself next time he can snore as loudly as he likes.

1963 Bassett Road machine-gun murders

The bullet-ridden bodies of Frederick George Walker and Kevin James Speight were found in a ransacked house at 115 Bassett Rd, Remuera. A team of 32 Auckland detectives began an immediate search that led to the arrest of Ron Jorgensen and John Gillies on New Year's Eve.

Frederick Walker was a 38-year-old commercial traveller; Kevin Speight, aged 26, was a seaman. Police concluded early in the investigation that the two victims were also sly-groggers– traders in illegal alcohol. The bootleg booze trade was a hot part of the Auckland criminal underground and seemed to be a key to the motive for the murders.

The coroners concluded that the men had been dead for two or three days when their bodies were found. The murder weapon was thought to be a .45-calibre machine gun. The man leading the police investigation was Detective Chief Inspector Robert Walton, who was to be Commissioner of Police from 1978 to 1983.

The first major lead came when future Prime Minister Robert Muldoon introduced Walton to a man he believed could assist with the case. It was this man who first pointed to John Gillies as a possible suspect. Although Gillies initially refused to answer questions, police work soon established a link between him and Jorgensen. The latter was unaware that he was under investigation until his arrest on 31 December. Gillies was arrested the same day.

The trial of the two men began on 24 February 1964. Although both denied the charges against them, Gillies did admit in court to having purchased a machine gun. After four hours of deliberation, the jury found both Jorgensen and Gillies guilty; each was sentenced to life imprisonment.

Jorgensen came to public attention again in 1984, following his release from prison, when his abandoned car was found at the bottom of a cliff near Kaikōura. Though his body was never found, he was declared dead in 1998. Rumours abounded about his whereabouts, with many believing he had become a police informant in Australia. His fate remains unknown.

Source: *www.nzhistory.net.nz/new-zealands-first-gang-style-killings-the-bassett-road-machine-gun-murders, (Ministry for Culture and Heritage), updated 16-Sep-2011*

Phil to the rescue

Later that day I was allowed a phone call. The only person I could call was Phil my boss from Refrigerated Appliances. I had to explain to him everything (all about jumping ship, my real name etc.) Phil was quite disappointed that I had not told him that I'd jumped ship, but after explaining my situation he said, he understood and realised it was my only way to find work. Within an hour he called with the company solicitor; he stood bail and had me released into his care.

He said "*I am quite happy to stand bail for you, because I know you are a good honest hardworking lad, who has been put in this position because of circumstances. I feel in my heart you will not let me down*". He was right I could no more let him down, than cut my two arms off. He was the reason that my stay in New Zealand had been so happy and carefree.

Helen was over the moon to see me and we quickly carried on as we had left off. She had heard the news about the riots but never for one-minute thought I was in there. On hearing of my arrest, Don moved out to another location with Pat. To this day don't know what happened to him. Maybe he is still out in New Zealand with his new identity.

I worked for Phil for a further two months. It proved to be a very busy period; we were installing huge refrigeration rooms in a new Woolworth store sixty miles outside Auckland. It was a small town called Huntley. Woolworth's also retailed food, so chest freezers and meat rooms added to the workload. We'd leave Auckland at first light and arrive back as the sun went down but such was the camaraderie it never felt like work, plus I continued learning new skills, with the added bonus of meeting really interesting people. I often bumped into various tradesmen from Liverpool, usually identified in the first instance by the unmistakable Liverpool twang echoing across the workplace. Some had come into New Zealand legally, but in the main many had, like me, jumped ship.

Chapter Nine – A Sad Farewell

Goodbye and tears

Early one afternoon I was on my knees putting the last bolt into the prefabricated corner section of a large meat fridge when Phil appeared at my side with a telegram in his hand. *"Come on"* he said. *"We have to get you back to Auckland. You are flying to Sydney tomorrow they have a ship for you"*. I felt really bad leaving Phil then as he was very busy and short staffed. Phil seemed quite okay about everything; he never seemed to get flustered, even when the pressure was on him. What a boss! He dropped everything and proceeded to drive me back to Auckland. He said he was at my disposal for the rest of the day, collecting clothes from the cleaners, paying outstanding bills like rent and visiting the many friends I had made in the short time I had been there. I wrote a note for the friends I could not contact. Phil's secretary was to have it typed up and distributed.

Just before driving me back to my home, he said he needed to call at the unit and collect the mail. He continued by asking me to go in with him and help him move some parts. We went into the darkened unit and as he switched the lights on, a loud cheer startled me. As my eyes adjusted to the brightness I was surprised to see all my friends and colleagues, even neighbours, applauding. He had even managed to round up two very close friends we were unable to contact during the day, all this done with him beside me most of the day. He must have enlisted some help, identifying my neighbours. It now made sense during his disappearing acts throughout the day (he was off finding telephones to arrange everything)

I felt a lump form in my throat and I was choked up and speechless. Helen ran up to me, threw her arms around me and started sobbing on my shoulder, I held her tight giving her time to compose herself, then gently led her to Phil's office, to sit and talk. After twenty minutes, we re-joined the party; and what a party it was, food, drink and music.

The music that emanated from a Parlophone record player, had been restricted to the Mersey Sound. The Beatles, Gerry and The Pacemakers, The Merseybeats and The Swinging Blue Jeans. These, I was told, came from Pete's collection, our honorary scouser!

However, it was me that felt honoured, I'd played a small part in bringing the Liverpool culture to the distant shores of New Zealand. I couldn't believe Phil had arranged all this for me, especially with his overloaded work schedule. Choking back my emotions, I found it very difficult to make a coherent speech.

What made matters worse, Helen's true feelings had surfaced, she couldn't stop sobbing all evening and confessed to me that she knew this day would come so hid her true feelings to mask any pain. I must admit I was really taken by her fun and positive attitude to life. Time was so short I felt heartbroken leaving her that way.

I was presented with a company calendar. My immediate work friends had put together a verse, each contributing a line, this will be etched on my mind for the rest of my life

It read:
> To Bob the lad who deserted a boat
> We bid a goodbye with a lump in our throat
> A toheroha hunter of no mean repute
> He caught a real whopper a fair Dinkum Beaut
> To his memory here a monument
> A wall that's half painted a mudguard that's bent
> All the best Bob wherever you may be
> Whether your name is Bob Yates or Tensing Ng

The party continued until the early hours of the morning, I had to be at Auckland Airport for 10am. I thanked everyone for their kindness and support. I had a hollow empty feeling inside, as Helen and I climbed into Phil's car for the journey back to the house. I watched as my colleagues and friends stood waving outside the darkened building. As the car moved off, they soon disappeared from sight. My eyes welled up as I fought back the tears. Helen turned to me and gently wiped one that had got away. We hugged and held hands in silence for the short journey home. After a sleepless night, Phil arrived early to take us to the airport.

Helen had talked about returning to Australia. She said, "*Once you've gone, there will be too many painful memories*". We had enjoyed many great times together, but we had only known each other for a few months and I hadn't for a moment realised her feelings ran so deep. We arrived at the airport deep in reflection. If only we had more time to sort things out. We agreed to keep in touch.

On the way to the airport, Phil said, "*I have a surprise for you, your workmates wanted to see you off, so I've closed the unit for the morning, they'll all be at the airport*". As the car pulled up, Pete greeted me with a slap on the back; he was far too macho to hug! "*What am I gonna do for my scouse lessons now mate?*" he asked. I laughed and replied, "*You are fully qualified to start your own scouse school*". Phil interjected "*Don't you dare, I don't want to lose a good engineer!*"

All the friendly banter continued over coffee, it helped to diffuse the emotions that had surfaced over the last 36 hours. A Quantas Airlines announcement broke the banter as my flight was called, instructing the passengers to make their way to the departure lounge. There were hugs all around then the ship's agent, who had been sitting quietly in the background, walked over, introduced himself and handed me a large brown envelope containing my papers. "*What ship am I joining?*" I enquired. "*I don't know, the agent in Sydney will have the details,*" he followed with, "*Good luck son, it seems that in a short time you have made some really good friends.*" Helen, Phil and Pete accompanied me to the gate. With all that was going on, I felt very reluctant to leave, everything was happening far to quickly. Helen held me tight and with tears running down her cheek, we kissed and she quietly sobbed into my shoulder. After a last long hug, we reluctantly tore ourselves apart. She then composed herself, stood back, eyes still full of tears and blew a kiss. She then turned for support from Phil. I had to be ushered through to the departure gate by the agent.

With the world on my shoulders and a lump in my throat, I headed into the departure lounge, I stopped, looked back once more, to see Phil placing a fatherly arm around Helen and gently talking to her. Tears did not come easily to me, but the emotion was such I was using more than my quota. Once again, I had to fight to hold them back.

In such a short time, all the friends and colleagues had become family to me and Phil certainly treated me as his own flesh and blood. Phil had also presented me with a gift wrapped present, under instructions not to open it until I had left Auckland. Phil said it's just a small token from us all to remind you of New Zealand.

I was torn leaving New Zealand, because although I had been there such a short time, just over four months in fact, I had experienced a beautiful young country with old fashioned values, its people were warm and friendly and full of love. But in the recesses of my mind was a feeling of excitement that I was making my way back to England and the family I loved and missed so much. In those days New Zealand seemed a whole world away from home and in times of despair I couldn't in my mind see a way of getting back. Now here was the opportunity to join a new ship and make my way home.

As the plane taxied down the runway I thought in a couple of months I should be home, I slowly opened the brown envelope...

Not good news

I couldn't believe it, I read it again, sure enough it was true they were sending me to Sydney to re-join the Cape Wrath, she was still out here after all those months. I really didn't want to go back on that ship and throughout the flight I was planning how to make my escape into Australia. Then reason told me it must be due home soon as it had already been away from the UK for eight months, heck it was probably on its way home now, but all the way across to Sydney my mind was a roller coaster of emotions, swinging one way then another.

When I opened the present, it revealed a symbol of New Zealand - A Maori Greenstone Tiki, known as a powerful good luck symbol, the tilted head represented "Thinking" the hand "Strength", the mouth is "Communication" and the heart is "Love".

Maori Greenstone Tiki

Underneath was an envelope with an extra month's salary and a collection fund from the workers. They had even converted the money to US dollars, typical of Phil he had thought of everything. The thought did cross my mind that Tiki wasn't working, or maybe I should have opened it first. Stupid I know. What was in the agent's envelope couldn't magically change.

The last few months had honed me into a very different person from the young naive lad that had deserted his ship in Auckland. I had grown both mentally and physically and the months ashore with its many highs and lows had transformed me into a much stronger person. I had grown not only in stature but also in self-belief. I felt that I could now take on anything that came my way; it had schooled me in new life awareness. As the plane touched down in Sydney, I felt different; I was a more robust person. With determination and my head and shoulders held high, I strode purposefully to the arrivals hall.

The passage from Auckland to Sydney probably represents the greatest turning point in my life. A new person was about to re-join the Cape Wrath.

Sydney

After I had passed through customs, the local shipping agent, who had been sent to make sure I didn't abscond in Australia, met me. By now, I had already in my mind decided to re-join the ship and was hoping to be home in a few months time.

En route to Australia

How wrong I was. The Cape Wrath lay at anchor in Sydney Harbour, basking in glorious sunshine. The Sydney Opera House had yet to be completed and the Sydney Harbour Bridge painted a wonderful picture in the deep blue waters of the Bay. We made our way to the vessel through the bustle of a busy harbour, a small-motorised boat being our means of transport.

The agent was obviously very proud of his city. He pointed out Taronga Park Zoo and other places of interest, but my mind was on other things, as the landscape seemed to darken, as the ship loomed closer. Seeing my apparent disinterest, he threw in the fact that the Cape Wrath's next port of call was Yokohama in Japan, calling in at various ports on the Japanese coast, from there she was bound for Ocean Island in the Pacific to load a cargo of phosphate for Bunbury, Western Australia. What was he trying to do, put me in a good mood? I realised then it would be some time yet before I saw home again. Would this nightmare never end?

Sydney Harbour 1965

It was with a heavy heart and deepening depression that I clambered the gangway. The chief officer met me at the top of the gangway and he escorted me to the Bridge. On boarding the ship, the strong smell of pungent diesel fuel pervaded my nostrils; the world seemed to darken with every step I took; the gloom covered me like a storm cloud. We called at the chief steward's cabin and then the three of us made our way midships to the Bridge. A couple of the engineers in oily overalls were servicing engine parts on the hot decks. They raised their heads and gave a cheer as I passed them, but I was in no mood for celebration.

The revelation that the Cape Wrath was to be my home for many months yet, angered and dismayed me. With a newfound strength I decided to fight my corner and my meeting with the Captain was a good place to start. What did I have to lose? At best the Captain could refuse to have me on board, then I would sail on the next available ship. At worst, I would have to re-join Cape Wrath.

As I entered, the Captain was leaning over some charts with his back to me. He boomed in his Scottish brogue "That was a very stupid thing you did back there lad" "I don't agree Captain" I replied, "After suffering the conditions on this ship I had a wonderful time in New Zealand, met some really genuine people and feel this has taught me a lot and enriched my life". I went on to explain my grievances, bringing the Chief Steward into the conversation, highlighting the food, stores and overtime situation. I said a huge part of the crew's unrest stemmed from lack of supplies and the cutting down on stores and loss of promised overtime. I also told him the comments about the bread and flour were ridiculous. I explained I was not happy re-joining the ship and unless things have changed, I would find a way to leave the ship again. He looked at me "You've changed lad. You have a lot of fire in your belly, but I'm prepared to put everything aside and start again, let bygones be bygones". In the next breath, he told me he was fining me a month's pay and deducting any costs relating to my repatriation. I paid the fare out of the gift from Phil, I wanted to settle my account and not start the trip, with the thought of working for nothing. After I had settled the bill, I was told I would not be allowed a sub or advance of my wages in the next port of call, Hong Kong. I wondered if he thought I was going to leave the ship again in because of my heritage! With my upbringing, I would be more likely to abandon ship in an English speaking country. Hong Kong was new to me. It was a place I'd always wanted to visit for reasons of my heritage. My father was born in Guangzhou (formerly known as Canton) in the Guangdong Province of Southern China. These days it is only about three hours by train or 40 minutes by plane from Hong Kong Island. To go to Hong Kong without access to money did not bear thinking about. I could have kicked myself; I should have let him wait for the money, keeping my dollars to use, as and when needed.

In the months I was away, a few more of the crew had jumped ship, including a junior officer. Consequently, there were some new faces on board. We had a new chief cook. The previous cook had paid off sick a few days after I had jumped ship in Auckland. Things had probably overwhelmed him, having the to do all the work himself. Working and living conditions had not improved and there were still rumblings of dissatisfaction. The ship still seemed to be split into ghettos as crewmembers formed clans and took sides. Drinking and fighting was still the order of the day. With no date of return to the UK forthcoming, the men's anger simmered, always on the edge of boiling point.

Next Stop Hong Kong...

Chapter Ten – The Far East

Hong Kong

For days, the prospect of seeing Hong Kong filled me with excitement. It was the place my father often talked about and the home of some of my ancestors. The Captain relented, allowed me a small advance and with a loan from some of my friends on board was able to raise enough money to explore this bustling city.

With my wife Jade on a trip to Hong Kong - 1990

I awoke at 4am to a view that, to this day, remains the most beautiful of all my memories. We were wending our way through many small islands on a very misty morning. The distant mountaintops seemed to hang in the clouds like an exquisite Chinese watercolour. The only sound was the rushing of water as the ship ploughed relentlessly on to Hong Kong. The occasional ship's horn disturbed this surreal quietness and the silent passing of ancient junks added to the atmosphere. As we got closer to Hong Kong the seas filled up with all manner of vessels, each on its own busy itinerary, crisscrossing each other. It was like a huge traffic junction without lights. I had never seen such a vast concentration of sea traffic. It became increasingly noisy as horns of every size and sound fought for space to make way to their predetermined destinations. I look back and wish that I'd had film for my camera to capture those moments. However, it left such an impression on me that I only need to close my eyes and it all comes back in startling detail.

We berthed on Kowloon side, not far from Tsim Sha Tsui, an ideal starting point for my explorations. When I left the dock, I had to face a line of rickshaw owners vying for trade. But, no, this was a place I had to explore on foot; to take my time, so I could update my father on my return, about the country of his birth. I made a beeline for the Star Ferry, to take me over to Hong Kong, for a few cents more I was able to travel on the upper deck, which offered a much better view. Locals, workers and the odd cage of live chickens mainly occupied the lower deck. The amazing views I was experiencing was an everyday occurrence to the locals, so mainly tourists or wealthy locals occupied the top deck. Leaving the ferry on Hong Kong side I made my way to Central and rode the funicular tram up its steep incline to Victoria Peak. I spent some time slowly wandering around the summit, stopping and admiring the views from every aspect during my trek around the 360-degree circumference. I leisurely made my way back down the mountain via the Peak Road. As I neared the bottom, the sound and bustle of the city grew louder.

I then caught a bus to Aberdeen harbour. On arrival, I felt I had walked onto a film set. An explosion of colours, sights, smells and sounds filled the early afternoon. I found a vantage point at a bar close to the waters edge, ordered a bottle of San Miguel beer then spent an hour or so taking in the sights. My eyes were on overtime as I tried to take in and absorb every tiny detail.

I watched sampans and junks ferrying tourists out to the Hong Kong Floating Restaurant, or offering harbour tours. Barefoot children six or seven years old with marvellous dexterity helped man the ancient houseboats, or sell souvenirs to fascinated tourists. Most of the sampan owners spent their lives living on the fruits of the tourist trade. As I walked around the harbour's edge, I saw weary fishermen offloading their catch of huge lobster and exotic fish; excited customers inspecting and haggling the best prices. No doubt many of the customers owned restaurants, or food stores that seemed to occupy a large percentage of retail space in this bustling city. I made my way back to Star Ferry and back to Kowloon, returning on the lower deck just to soak in the atmosphere.

Evening was drawing in, as I headed up towards Mong Kok. The City was alive and heaving! I'd never experienced such a huge concentration of people. I fought my way up Nathan Road, briefly visiting the Jade market at Yau Ma Tei, but found it to be mainly overpriced and garish. I continued taking in the sights, colours and smells that seemed to seep from every direction. Suddenly and quite unexpectedly, I was caught in a monsoon-like rainfall. How the streets emptied; the occupants taking shelter among the thousands of retail outlets or covered market areas. I was amazed as umbrellas appeared as if by magic and residents just carried on as if nothing was different.

Twenty minutes later the pavements were dry and only side streets and recesses showed any evidence of the recent downpour. Night-time Kowloon seemed to take on a whole new personality. It became more colourful; neon signs hung from every available space. In places this created a seedy atmosphere, pimps and prostitutes plied for trade, copy watch sellers opened their Jackets to expose all brands of fake watches. "A store in a jacket" I recall thinking.

Phrases I remember:

> *"You want Rolex, or Omega Mr!";*
> *"You come with me Johnny? I give you best time!"*
> *"You American? Plenty girls for you, very clean!"*
> *"You follow me, my girls just like film star!"*

"You want new suit, or maybe shirt very cheap!"
"New suit two hours!"

I made my way to the Ladies Market, well known for bargains, such things as electronics, clothes, souvenirs, etc. I bought half a dozen tee shirts and a watch that stopped working two days after we left Hong Kong. "Waterproof to 50 metres" it boasted; at the first sign of steam it clouded up, then the minute hand fell off. Food stalls offered all kinds of aromas and delicacies, tanks of live fish, squid, shellfish and even snakes littered the sidewalks inviting guests to pick what they wanted freshly cooked. This was quite alien to me and I couldn't find the heart to condemn another creature to death, besides I couldn't stomach the thought of eating something I'd watched swimming around a tank moments before. I settled for some dim sum and a pot of china tea. The sound of clattering Mah-jong tiles escaped from many doorways and open windows, accompanied by raised voices that to the untrained ear would mistakenly attribute to arguing. The humidity and hours of walking began taking its toll and in the early hours of the morning, as my legs tired, I wearily made my way back to the ship. A quick shower did nothing to alleviate my tiredness and before my head hit the pillow, I was in a deep sleep.

It would have been nice to venture across the border to visit the place of my father's birth but owing to immigration restrictions, it was not possible. Later on in life, I have found the opportunity on two occasions to do just that and have even met some long-lost relatives. It was such a brief visit; far too fleeting to see even a tiny bit of this sprawling, hectic city.

Two days later we departed for Yokohama, Japan.

Japan

My most enduring memory about Japan is, "Honesty and good manners". I was informed by members of the crew who had been there months before, that I didn't have to lock my cabin whilst in port. The reason was, that anyone caught stealing would result in total loss of face. That would stigmatise them and family members for the rest of their lives. The port authority also ruled that if there was any evidence of theft, all members of the ship's gang would be instantly dismissed!

After losing a wristwatch of much sentimental value from my cabin on a previous trip to South America, I took this with a pinch of salt. I even thought it was a wind up by my so-called shipmates, so I continued to lock my door.

The dock workers, who incidentally had impeccable manners, if you had to pass them in the alleyway, would sometimes sit outside my cabin to eat lunch from small cardboard boxes with tiny wooden chopsticks, always cleaning up after themselves. All around me, cabin doors were left open and before long, my cabin too became open to the world as I started to feel guilty. I was insulting this impeccable-mannered race by not trusting them. My trust in them was never challenged.

A typical cassette tape recorder

The latest gadget in Japan at that time was a Philips Cassette Player. The bosun had bought one in Yokohama on a previous visit. Even in those days, I was a gadget freak. It was so tiny in comparison to the cumbersome reel-to-reel Alba tape recorder that we had at home. I made it my business to seek one out on arrival in Yokohama. I headed into the city and made my way to the largest department store only to find they had sold out. I ended up buying a musical jewellery box with a twirling ballerina, something I knew my mother would love. I left the store and tried other places but they had all sold out. I was informed that a stock of Panasonic players were due in the next few days. Unfortunately we were due to sail early the next morning and I returned to the ship highly disappointed.

Gloom and a sickening sensation followed on the heels of disappointment, as I realised I had lost my wallet, and with it approximately four weeks' wages, the money I had saved to buy presents, and the elusive cassette recorder. Our next port of call, Osaka, was very industrial, so I had little chance of finding one there.

I caught the Bullet train to Tokyo, introduced in 1964 called the Shinkansen, which means new main line; with a reputation of attaining speeds of 135mph. The guard spoke very good English, as he proudly boasted about the Shinkansen. He went on to tell us the train had only achieved 120mph on this particular day, due to weather conditions. Everything flashed past the windows; it was a wonderful experience, and I felt I was part of history in the making. We only had two hours to look around owing to the short stay in port so I put my search for the cassette player on the back burner.

The Shinkansen

Back at the Cape Wrath, I received the news that we were returning to Yokohama after a short stop in Chiba. I was hopeful that the store would have had time to restock. Please bear with me if I seem to be rambling on, but there is a point to this story, which will become clear over the next few paragraphs.

I made my way back to the department store, rode the elevator to the second floor and the counter that I had made enquiries at on my first visit. The same petite Japanese lady with the beautiful, smiling porcelain like face I encountered on my previous trip, served me again. Although it had been three weeks since my last visit, she remembered me and asked me to "*please wait*" while she summoned her manager. "*He speak English very good*", she said.

The manager appeared, looking very dapper in a black double-breasted suit, white shirt and sporting a black tie with a bright gold company logo. After the usual bowing introduction he told me his name and said, "*I remember you*" and then followed with "*Did you lose something last time?*" I couldn't think, "*Money maybe*" he prompted. Then the light bulb came on "*Ah yes my wallet*" I exclaimed. He asked me to describe it and its contents. He then went off to retrieve it from the stores safe. I couldn't believe it. I offered a reward. He refused to accept and said, "*Our reward is to see you reunited with your lost belongings*".

My day, in complete contrast to my last visit, ended in finally purchasing the elusive cassette recorder and having my wallet returned intact.

I had great trouble finding cassettes to supply my new toy; there were plenty of Japanese recordings available, but nothing to suit my taste. I had to settle for Johnny Cash gospel songs and Frank Sinatra hits until the cassette recordings caught on in The UK many months later. I would lie in my bunk at night listening, I would often wake up in the middle of the night with the large headphones still on and the end of the tape hissing in my ears. That Johnny Cash cassette gave birth to my interest in country music, which I still enjoy to this day.

The abiding memory of my visit to Japan will remain with me for the rest of my life. A nation of hardworking, innovative and honest people; I am sure there are many exceptions, but I can only take as I find.

I feel that the innate honesty of its people has all to do with upbringing, family and loss of face incurred with any wrongdoing. This is true in any race in the world, provided the family structure and guidance is in place. I was fortunate that in Japan, I personally found it in abundance.

Helen and I had corresponded by airmail. I would write informing her of our next port and arrive often finding three or four blue airmail letters waiting for me. She had a wonderful way with words, but reading her letters gave me pangs of guilt, that she was feeling so down. It was rumoured we may call at Christchurch South Island on the way to Australia. Helen promised me if that happened, she would meet me there. It was almost five hundred miles, quite a distance that would entail a train and ferry journey. We had left so many things unsaid, owing to my hasty departure; it would have been good to tie up any loose ends. Sadly, it was only rumour and regrettably we never did meet again.

Chapter Eleven – Back to Australia

Shark

We dropped anchor early afternoon in Cleveland Bay, just off Magnetic Island Townsville. One of the officer cadets had spotted a shark off the bow end, all eyes scouring the calm blue waters, watching for any more signs. After lunch, we washed down the benches and swilled down the galley before going back to our cabins for a quick change into trunks and grabbing a towel, then made our way to the after end to do a bit of sunbathing. It was a very hot humid day with a slight breeze bringing welcome relief from the sweltering early afternoon sun. The poop deck provided very little shade.

The Bosun, ship's carpenter (chippie) and cook decided to do a bit of shark fishing. They defrosted a large piece of bloodied liver and secured it to a butcher's hook. A rope from the chain locker completed the fishing line. One end of the line was secured to the winch and the bait and line was then thrown overboard. What happened next had us all rolling about with laughter.

To entice the sharks, the cook tried to throw a bucket full of galley slops and blood overboard. As he was about to let go of the bucket, he slipped and slid, landing on his backside, the upturned bucket planted itself firmly on his head and the entire smelly contents slithered down over his head and shoulders. After a long soak in the shower, a new nickname "*bucket*" was born. We ribbed him continually. It wasn't "*Hey cook*" anymore, it became "*Hey bucket*". After a few weeks this started to wear a bit thin and after constant ribbing, it ended up with the cook offering one burly sarcastic able seaman out on deck to put an end to all the taunting. The cook, who was half the size of the seaman and quite scrawny and advanced in years, knocked him clean out after about three minutes. It turned out the cook in his younger days had been a schoolboy-boxing champion. From there on his title went back to chief cook or Doc, a seafaring term for the ships cook.

However, I digress. Later that afternoon they managed to hook an eleven-foot tiger shark. They had to use the winch to haul it on board and it seemed a lot bigger than eleven feet. It was only later when we managed to get a tape on it that size was confirmed 11' 2" to be precise. I felt it was cruel and implored the lads to let it go. It put up tremendous fight and half an hour later it was lying very still, but with a sudden thrash, it knocked the bosun off his feet!

In the meantime, the pilot had boarded. We raised the anchor and made our way alongside. A shock was yet to come.

The Port Health Authority fined the company the equivalent of £200 for bringing the bloodied carcass of a shark into port. They said quite rightly that blood dripping over the side would have the potential to attract other sharks into the bay endangering the local populace. They gave us three hours to have the carcass removed and disposed of twenty miles away from Townsville. The ships agent arranged everything at a cost equivalent to £60. The captain went ballistic! He summoned everyone on the poop deck to the bridge. That included me, who was only sunbathing. The captain read the riot act then docked the total cost of the fine and removal, equally shared between the seven of us, almost forty pounds each. I was not very happy, as my monthly pay was only £54.10d.

The regrettable thing was a shark had lost its life, for the sake of a souvenir fin that the ship's carpenter mounted on a mahogany stand.

Aground

On the way to Esperance, we were informed that we would be the first ship to dock on the brand new land backed berth. A 3425-foot breakwater had been built and the basin and entrance channel had been dredged to allow ships of our size alongside. The then Premier of Western Australia Sir David Brand and local dignitaries, complete with brass band would welcome us in. The pilot clambered aboard and we proceeded to negotiate our way up the narrow newly dredged channel. Just inside the breakwater, with a crunch we ran aground blocking the entrance. The small pilot boat put-putted its way over and tried to push us off. A comical sight as the boat was nothing more than a small day boat. At the time, tugs were not available.

In the distance we could hear the band starting up obviously unaware of our predicament. We kept turning the screw over, the water turned a murky brown as we disturbed the bottom. Eventually, the captain decided that we stayed put until the tide rose. About three hours later we were able to make our way in and divers went down to check that no damage had been done. They reported that all is well. Luckily, we never made contact with the rocky bottom. Not a great start to the opening of a new port, but at least the band got some overtime. The hilarious sight of the day boat trying to push us off the sandbank has no doubt been recounted many times over the years.

We unloaded some of the phosphate and according to research we loaded grain. I don't recall that, but it was a long time ago. We then gingerly made our way out of Esperance. Our next port of call was Bunbury.

The impetus for the new land-backed berth and breakwater was the opening of the Esperance Coastal Plain for agriculture and the discovery of nickel by Western Mining Cooperation at Kambalda, although there was talk about the suitability of the site for land-backed berths at the 1915 Royal Commission into the opening of the Mallee for agriculture.

Dignitaries and locals gathered at the Port on November 19, 1965, to hear the then Premier of Western Australia, Sir David Brand, officially open the berth and the first grain rolled off the conveyors into the MV Cape Wrath.

Grain carrying vessels, however, were getting bigger and the Esperance grain berth with an alongside depth of 10.5 metres was only capable of loading to about 40,000 tonnes. Larger ships had to sail to Albany or Bunbury to top up.
Source: *Esperance Ports Newsletter June 2010*

Bunbury

Bordered by the Indian Ocean, Bunbury has an almost Mediterranean climate. The end of November heralded the arrival of the summer season. Crystal blue waters welcomed us into Bunbury. As it was early morning, temperatures were creeping up and the sky threatened a hot day. I had the afternoon off so a few of us planned a little sunbathing on the nearby beautiful white sands. By mid morning, the deserted beach was slowly attracting the local populace into the cool inviting waters. One able seaman, binoculars glued to his eyes, spent the morning giving a running commentary on the numbers of Sheilas he'd spotted throwing down beach towels.

The cook and I decided to cool him down. We set up the sea hose, filled buckets with ice water, thoroughly doused him first with buckets of water and then prevented his escape with the powerful sea hose. This was done in a playful mood but unfortunately, in the melee his binoculars were washed overboard. A couple of the lads taking an opportunity to cool down dived overboard on the pretence of searching for them. Half a dozen more of the crew followed suit.

With thoughts of Tampa still on my mind, I stayed on board. Not for long though. The ogling seaman and two others thought it about time I got over my fear and threw me over the side. It was about twenty-five feet deck-to-water. I made impact backside first; swallowed a mouthful of oily water and within three minutes was climbing up the pier. I didn't mind swimming in nice clear waters but not in the residue of dirty waters close to the ships side.

We made our way to the beach. The sand was like talcum powder, or it certainly felt that way after the shores I remember from back home. The bright blue skies and sparkling warm waters made a couple of hours seem like minutes. All too soon, we had to make our way back to the ship. A string of buoys linked together with a shark net, protected the beach and the swimmers against marauding sharks. There had been quite a few shark attacks locally. The most common was the white pointer shark, which was known as the great white. Tiger sharks were also in abundance.

One of the crew found a hole in the netting and swam through with the intention of swimming round the bay and back to the ship. The local coastguard picked him up and severely reprimanded him before bringing him back to the ship. Warning notices were posted in every mess room and on the gangway. Some good did come out of it though. The broken net was located and the next day an inspection team was sent out to survey and fix any holes.

We never did retrieve the binoculars. The cook and I clubbed together and bought him a new pair in the next port.

Seas in turmoil

On leaving Bunbury the weather was calm. It was a strange calmness; the skies were heavy with a thunderous presence. I stood on deck leaning on the railing and the cooling sea spray offered me temporary relief from the suffocating heat of the galley. The deep thumping of the ship's engines and the whisper of rushing water as the ship carved it's way forward seemed to hold me in a trance. I stared out into the vast oppressive blackness before me. We were now heading into open sea. The bosun sidled up to me, disturbing my thoughts. He rolled a cigarette and said, "*A word of warning, the radio officer has just informed me that freak weather lies ahead*". The deck crew had been instructed to batten down hatches and make secure and stow anything that could move. The sky ahead looked ominously black and a much heavier rain started to pepper my face. I retired to my cabin to stow anything that was likely to be tossed around. All crew had been mustered to make safe their working stations.

I was put in charge of the fridges. Sides of beef and lamb carcasses had to be secured to the steel shelving and the fruit and vegetable boxes lashed together to hinder movement. The chief cook and galley boy took care of the galley, lining shelving with damp sheets to stop plates and utensils moving about. I had never witnessed such preparation. There must be an exceptionally bad storm brewing. During the evening, the weather steadily declined. This was the start of horrendous conditions as the captain tried to navigate around the swirling typhoon. We had to navigate south to avoid a number of Tornados. The Cape Wrath creaked and groaned as the sea and conditions tossed her around like a cork. Cooking became impossible. We staggered around the galley, spending all our time and energy trying to stay on our feet, continually having to stow items that had come adrift. We substituted hot food for cold meats and salad and tinned pilchards. It was impossible to make decent bread as the dough refused to rise with all the buffeting.

As the days went on, the disgruntled crew started demanding hot food. The chief cook, under pressure, decided to attempt to boil some eggs on the oil-burning stove. To do this we had to use a very large cauldron with about 4 inches of water, immersed in this were eight tea towels with two dozen eggs laid on top to stop them moving and bashing against the side of the cauldron. Iron bars slotted into the stove to hold the cauldron in place. All was going well, so we set up the second batch of eggs.

A terrific bang resonated as a huge wave caught the port side of the ship - all hell broke loose. The cauldron jumped the rails, ejecting its contents like missiles across the deck. I was hanging on for dear life to a galley bench when my leg felt the brunt of the hot, but thankfully not yet boiling water. This threw me off balance and sent me surfing on my backside across the galley. Plates jumped the dish racks, smashing and sliding on the deck. The steel cupboard doors flew open

Stove with wire stays, unlike the heavy metal bars on the Cape Wrath

ejecting pots, pans and kitchen utensils into the melee. Before we had time to tidy up the mess another array of galley implements would rain down on us. All this time the cook had managed to hang onto the galley door, but he had taken a bad knock to his ankle.

On my fourth or fifth slide across the galley, he succeeded in grabbing my T-shirt enabling me to secure a position across the galley step. We managed to fight our way out of the mess that was previously a well-ordered galley. The chief cook retired to his cabin obviously in great pain and left me to clean up the mess when the seas calmed. I had small lacerations on my hands and back from sliding on the broken plates, but generally, I escaped what could have been some serious injuries. So it was back to serving up cold cuts, salads and hard cake like bread for the next few days.

Chapter Twelve – South Africa

Cape Town

I awoke to the sound and vibration of the anchor leaving the ship. The sea was very calm and as I drew back my curtains, the harsh sunlight almost blinded me; it was so bright at this early hour. I walked onto deck and was filled with awe seeing the Table Top Mountain in all her splendour.

I showered and went down into the galley to prepare for the

Cape Town 1965 – Table Mountain

day ahead. I was alone in this task, as the chief cook had taken to drinking again after the heavy weather incident. Alcohol had become part of the cook's daily itinerary and although the captain had stopped his supplies, he still managed to find plenty from his drinking buddies. I was left to run the galley along with a young catering boy from South Wales. By 10.30am, we had cleaned down after breakfast and the catering boy and I decided to have a coffee on the poop deck. As we stood admiring the view, a school of porpoise broke the surface about sixty feet away. They skipped in unison around the ship as if to put on a display just for us. After a few minutes, they disappeared. We scoured the waters but to no avail. We were just about to go back to work when not thirty feet from the after end of the ship a whale rose majestically out of the water and came crashing down again.

This drenched the galley boy who in shock dropped his coffee cup over the side. Later in the day one of the deckhands shouted "*Shark*" and sure enough we were treated to a display of fins cutting through the crystal blue waters. What an introduction to South Africa!

We took on stores at Cape Town and I was presented with a major problem with the flour. It was obviously old and of bad quality as it was overrun with weevils. I had to sieve every bag meticulously before making bread or baking. It was a soul-destroying job, especially in the hot weather. I made all the bread by hand in a large stainless steel tub. It was going to be a long job as we had taken on board 150 x 56lb bags. The cook and I tried when we could, to dump badly infected bags over the side. We had to do this in the dead of night from the after end. We found that freezing the bags prior to sieving the flour made the job a lot easier. But we knew that the sooner we got rid, the sooner we would be able to replace it with hopefully weevil-free stock. We were not happy subjecting the crew to the possibility of eating bugs. In today's world, flour in that state would be condemned.

When we requested more flour, the chief cook and I were once again hauled to the bridge to explain how we had used so much flour. I informed the captain and chief steward, that I was losing quite a lot during sieving, due to the high infestation. He said, "*A few weevils won't kill anyone. Just sieve half the bag*". Their logic was starting to drive me mad. I noticed that the officers hardly ate bread or pastries. We managed to dump about thirty bags without detection.

A weevil is any beetle from the Curculionoidea superfamily. They are usually small, less than 6 millimetres (0.24 in) and herbivorous. There are over 60,000 species in several families, mostly in the family Curculionidae (the true weevils). Some other beetles, although not closely related, bear the name "weevil", such as the biscuit weevil (Stegobium paniceum), which belongs to the family Anobiidae.

Many weevils are damaging to crops. The grain or wheat weevil (Sitophilus granarius) damages stored grain. The boll weevil (Anthonomus grandis) attacks cotton crops. It lays its eggs inside cotton bolls and the young weevils eat their way out.

Weevils are often found in dry foods including nuts and seeds, cereal and grain products, such as pancake mix. In the domestic setting, they are most likely to be observed when a bag of flour is opened. Their presence is often indicated by the granules of the infested item sticking together in strings, as if caught in a cobweb.

Source: *Wikipedia, the free encyclopaedia.*

Durban

After three days spent in Cape Town discharging cargo, we set sail for Durban with the news that we were going into dry dock, as the ship's hull needed some work doing after our grounding in Esperance. Speculation amongst the crew that we had left Australia and sailed across the Southern Ocean, one of the most unforgiving seas, with a damaged hull was rife. Mess room gossip of what could have happened, particularly with the bad weather we had encountered, sent a chill through my bones. Christmas and the New Years was upon us. It was likely to be a six to eight week stay.

Robert aged 19 years

Durban was very similar to Cape Town, but walking around the city the air was pulsating with uneasiness and underlying tension. There was a great deal of unrest between the black population and the Afrikaans community. Cape Town was going through a big

157

transition segregating the blacks into the homelands, mainly slum areas, leaving the city mainly white. Expectation was that this was filtering through to Durban, hence the anger and distrust.

We unloaded some cargo then moved into dry dock. The expected time in dry dock meant our meagre wages didn't go far. The Seaman's mission became a godsend (sorry about the pun) but for value for money, it couldn't be beaten.

We would play pool or darts and the odd game of cribbage. Some of the lads got into gambling, losing huge amounts thus finding they'd lost so much that at the end trip, on collecting payoff, they would have to pay most of it to creditors. I personally got caught out for a weeks wages, but it taught me a very valuable lesson in life, to this day I only bet on the occasional football match or the Grand National. As the voyage went on it became clear that some of the crew worked in teams to alleviate the less savvy of us of hard earned cash. It was a bitter pill to swallow that led to many mess room brawls.

I was surprised to see a rickshaw; it was a totally unexpected sight as I didn't associate rickshaws with South Africa. I was window-shopping in Durban and in the reflection of the window, appeared a huge Zulu warrior resplendent in full tribal costume and chanting loudly. He was engaged in throwing himself up and down in the air holding onto the brightly decorated rickshaw. Quite a shock when your minds miles away! The expression on my face must have been a picture. It was his way of touting for trade. I thought, "*If he's not careful he'll kill off any prospective customers*".

The time in dry dock meant some of the crew didn't have a lot to do so excess drinking started to raise its ugly head again. One guy, a huge able seaman, had been nicknamed Lurch after a character from the television series, "*The Adams Family*". He was a nasty piece of work when under the influence of drink and on a few occasions had picked on other members of the crew, started a fight and due to his size, would usually leave his victim in a bloodied heap on the floor.

It was a very humid day and I was working alone in the galley. The chief cook had gone on a drinking binge and the galley boy had stayed ashore from the night before. I was running the galley single-handed. Cooking, baking and cleaning, with a crew of 37 it took me every minute to keep things on time. I'd been in the galley since 5.30 that morning, It was now 3.30pm and I had just finished washing down after lunch. I had a quick shower, discarding my sweat soaked tee shirt. A change of work clothes seemed to give me new energy; I was feeling a lot fresher but there was no time to rest. I had to prepare some cold meats for salad that night.

Lurch appeared; his large head and shoulders filling the galley hatch. "*Hey cook! get me some effing lunch!*" "*Sorry Lurch*" I replied, "*Everything has been cleaned down now. I'll give you some cold meat and you can make yourself a sandwich in the mess room*". His face contorted with rage. "*If you don't get me some hot food I'll come in there and beat you to a f...ing pulp!*" he snarled.

I tried to reason with him but his bullying attitude only got worse, he seemed to take reasoning as a sign of weakness.

My father, an ex merchant seaman himself, spoke to me at some length about the types of characters I was likely to meet and the pitfalls if I came up against bullying. He said, "*Never let a bully see you are afraid, stand up to them. On a ship you can't walk away or hide, if you are cornered, make sure you hit them first; aim for the nose and hit as hard as you can*".

The adrenaline was rising; I was in no mood to back down, besides he had presented himself as a perfect target wedged in the hatch. I was slicing a joint of beef with a Chinese cleaver face to face with him. Suddenly, the survival instinct kicked in. I reached for the sliding hatch above his head, released the catch and jammed it down over his neck. I waved the cleaver in front of his face and shouted at him in the angriest voice I could muster, "*If you come near me you'll f...ing get this*!" Swearing, I rarely used, but I think it helped to put a bit of menace in my attitude. His face drained of colour and he seemed to sober up immediately. "*Only joking cook,*" he exclaimed as he tried to wriggle back out of the hatch. I kept him trapped for a few more minutes, until he gave me assurances that this was the end of the matter. It had done the trick, as he never bothered me again and on the occasions that our paths crossed, treated me in a respectful manner.

I found out later that an able seaman had witnessed the whole episode from the galley doorway. He soon spread it around the ship and the message went out that you don't mess with the second cook, so in many ways I believe that episode smoothed the path for me. He carried on bullying other members of the crew. He was eventually discharged for attacking one of the junior officers with a tin of paint. I was told that this incident marked the end of his seagoing days. Dad's advice had paid off, but when I look back it could have ended rather differently.

I began to realise that to survive at sea you had to stand your ground, perhaps even act a lot stronger than you physically were, otherwise you'd get walked over.

Apartheid

I was warned about apartheid in South Africa. I was told I had to be careful where I went. Being of mixed Chinese heritage, I was classed as coloured, unlike people of Japanese origin who were classed as white. Apparently, it was because Japan and South Africa had very strong trade links with each other.

Coming from Britain, this was completely repugnant to me and most of the crew, so I disregarded any warnings and well meaning advice and went ashore with shipmates and visited places classed as whites only. As far as I was concerned my whole upbringing was English, I didn't feel it was right that any human should be categorised and treated differently. I was damned if I was going to let apartheid tell me that I could not socialise with my shipmates.

I didn't encounter any problems going ashore. It has on occasions been said that I look more Italian or Spanish than Chinese, so I am sure that helped. But I was very wary of being asked to produce my seaman's identity card. With my surname being Ng, it would have given the game away.

The following article from Roddy Bray's Guide to Cape Town

In the 1960s Prime Minister Hendrik Verwoerd pursued a policy of 'Grand Apartheid', which established 'independent tribal homelands', such as the Transkei. The plan made it possible to exclude blacks from a right to live in 'South Africa'. A rule was imposed in 1965 by which African workers had to return to their 'homeland' at the end of an employment contract, then re-apply to work in the Cape Town area. This was supposed to prevent any growth in the numbers of black 'permanent residents' in the city.

During the 1960s the South African economy grew rapidly and while this helped keep a lid on protest, it raised the need for more black labour. The government, however, refused to issue more passes for Africans to work in Cape Town, on the grounds that the Western Cape should become a 'safe white homeland' as well as offer 'a future for coloured people'.

Black people 'endorsed out' of Cape Town were sent to 'resettlement camps' in the Eastern Cape where they lived in atrocious conditions. Within Cape Town's townships, municipal beer halls and liquor stores were opened in spite of local opposition. The sale of alcohol helped to finance the enforcement of apartheid.

Yet, in spite of the influx regulations Cape Town still grew considerably. Official figures show an increase in the 'legal' African population from 70,000 in 1960 to 160,000 in 1974 and it is estimated that there were a further 90,000 'illegals'. The springing up of more shanty-towns north and south of the airport showed that apartheid was failing to achieve its aims.

For more interesting articles see: Roddy Bray's Guide to Cape Town.

I was shocked to find the beaches segregated, different buses for whites and non-whites, even benches had signs stating blankes (whites) only. The fact that they operated segregated ambulances really brought home to me how oppressed the non-white community must feel. Such a beautiful country to be stained by apartheid...

I did encounter a bit of personal trouble regarding my status as coloured in Durban. We looked forward to Friday nights as it was dance night at the Seaman's Mission and a cluster of local girls from the church would provide us with female company. All above board and respectable, these girls came from good families and were chaperoned home after the dance.

A couple of apartheid signs

Over the weeks, I formed a very close relationship with one of the girls that I met at the dance. All agreed Stella was the belle of the dance floor and the lads queued to dance with her. Stella was very bubbly and pretty and judging by the way that she graced the dance floor had obviously had lessons. I could not dance to save my life, so sat watching as others took to the floor. She must have taken pity on me as I sat there alone, with only a glass of coke to keep me company. After a few dances she came over to my table and asked me "*Don't you dance?*" I said "*it's not easy with two left feet*" She laughed and replied, "*Come on I'll teach you a few steps*". I didn't need to be asked twice, I joined her on the floor followed by envious glances from my shipmates. We danced together all evening. When some of the lads tried an excuse me, she said, *"I'm so sorry I'm in the middle of lessons"*. We carried on with hardly any improvement on my part. I couldn't believe my luck. Here was I, probably the worst dancer in the room and certainly not the best looking, having the attention that all my shipmates craved. We'd really enjoyed each other's company and arranged, against Mission rules, to go to the cinema the next Sunday evening.

The following day one of the rejected crewmembers said to me *"Does Stella know your coloured?"* I angrily argued with him and a scuffle ensued but was quickly broken up by the bosun. Just as well really as he was a much bigger and stronger man than me, his party piece was doing one-arm press-ups. I certainly would have come off worse. This same man had criticised the politics of apartheid for weeks. He then threatened to tell Stella. The bosun shouted at him *"Don't be an arsehole, leave the lad alone."*

That night I didn't sleep knowing it was only right I reveal my 'coloured status' to Stella. We met in our usual place, just outside the bus station. She ran towards me, threw her arms around me, and then said, *"I know it's only been a few days but I've missed you"*. A lump formed in my throat as I contemplated a possible sudden end to our relationship. All through the movie, I felt as if I had the whole world on my shoulders. I kept rolling scenarios over in my mind, how would I broach the subject. The last thing I wanted was to hurt her, she was in such a happy mood tonight. Halfway through the film, I felt Stella's hand tighten in mine, *"What's the matter?"* she said, *"You are not watching this film are you?"*

I suddenly realised I didn't have a clue what the film was about. My thoughts had been completely taken over by the task in hand. I gently cupped her face and said *"Stella we need to talk"*. Tears welled up in her eyes and slowly rolled down her cheek, *"Don't you want to see me again?"* she said. *"Nothing could be further from the truth"* I replied. *"Let's go *for a coffee*". We made our way out of the cinema into the cool evening air, well before the film had ended. I held her close as I guided her to our favourite ice cream and coffee bar. We found a softly lit quiet alcove, away from the evening bustle and noisy patrons. With great trepidation and a fear of rejection, I haltingly explained my situation.

She put both hands in mine looked into my eyes, and quietly said, "*Not everyone in South Africa agrees with apartheid and certainly our church group is not in favour. It must be hard for you to understand, as you are no different from me. Don't worry about it, I enjoy your company and love your great sense of humour. So good riddance to everyone else.*" I felt elated she had taken it so well. It was as if a huge weight was lifted from my shoulders. We chatted so long the coffee bar owner had to ask us to leave because it was after closing time.

The last bus had gone, so I ordered a taxi and rode home with her, leaving her at the end of her road. In the excitement I suddenly realised I didn't have enough money on me to pay for a taxi back to the ship. I walked the five miles or so, what did it matter, I had renewed vitality and a spring in my step, I suddenly felt as if I was floating on a cloud.

I suppose I was lucky that I had come to no harm, as walking alone through the area around the docks at two in the morning was not a done thing. I was informed the next day by the chief officer, that two Danish seamen had been badly beaten up and robbed only days before.

I was so glad that I had cleared the air and delighted she wanted to continue seeing me. We managed to see each other surreptitiously on three more occasions.

Sadly, it all came to an end when the jealous crewmember did confront Stella. Being forewarned she told him to mind his own business. But when her parents arrived to pick her up and take her home, he told them.

The following Sunday Stella didn't make our arranged meeting. I waited for over an hour and felt an aching in my heart as it became apparent in my mind she had been grounded. I prayed that by Friday she would reappear. Friday came and Stella was nowhere to be seen.

One of her friends secretly passed a letter from her, informing me that her family had barred her from going to the mission. She said she thought the world of me, her family said that if things had developed, Apartheid offered no prospect for a happy future for either of us. She went on to say:

"I am crying as I write this, sorry for the smudges, I am so sorry I have been banned from making contact with you again. Thank you for the fun carefree and special moments we've had together, you will always have a place in my heart, please look after yourself,

Love Stella xxxx".

I was devastated. I read the letter repeatedly, trying to understand what made me different. It was never an issue in England, ok I had endured a bit of racism, as a schoolboy but nothing on this scale. In my eyes, it was evil that segregated and tore people and families apart. I wondered how could a nation grow strong without the harmony and backing of its entire people. We were just two young people enjoying each other's company, far too early to think about a permanent relationship. I was upset that I could not answer her letter having no address. It would have been nice if I could have thanked her for the sunshine and happiness she stamped on my short stay in her beautiful, but tarnished land.

This episode in my life gave me a completely new perspective on one of the many cultures I had witnessed. To break up in such circumstances was to a young lad almost akin to bereavement, it left me feeling hollow and empty for many months after. Being in port for such a long time, romance beckoned for some of the crew and a few hearts were broken when it came time to leave. I often wonder what happened to

Stella and hope that she went on to lead a wonderful and fruitful life that her delightful personality deserved.

As for the jealous crewmember, he didn't do himself any favours acting the way he did; the girls at the mission would have nothing to do with him. And I was still cooking food for him... but I'd better leave it there!

Chapter Thirteen - Homeward Bound

Going home!

I left Durban with great sadness and a heavy heart and with only the thought of a possible return home to comfort me. We were on our way to Madagascar and then on through the Suez Canal to Genoa. Some of the lads predicted that we would get paid off there, while other rumour merchants said that on the grapevine the word was that the ship was picking up a cargo for Tampa again. Madagascar must have made no impression on me, as I can remember almost nothing about it, or maybe my mind was on fast forward as I willed the ship on its way home. We made our way through the Suez Canal without incident, although at that time it was the centre of war rumblings and talk of closure.

All the way to Genoa, we suffered highs and lows as rumour fed rumour as to our possible discharge in Italy. Right up to two days before docking, we could not elicit any clue as to what was happening. Finally, the long awaited news came; we were to be discharged and flown home. The news transformed the crew into party mood, the gripes and hostilities seemingly forgotten. The atmosphere was almost the same as the day we left Birkenhead. Once in port, some of us had to work on-board for three extra days, allowing the company time to send replacements. Those that were surplus to requirements left the ship the day after arrival. I watched as the chief cook struggled down the gangway to a waiting taxi. The holding crew had to eat and I had been elected to look after the catering side, with only a third of the crew on board, the job did not stretch me.

The next few days seemed to stand still, as the excitement of returning home crowded my thoughts. Those few days in port, waiting for my replacement, seemed like weeks. With a skeleton crew, we had such a small workload, so I busied myself making sure everything was spick and span, so that the relieving crew had nothing to complain about. I left the ship in the knowledge it was in far better condition than the state we endured when I joined her.

On paying off in Genoa my discharge book was stamped with a VNC Seaman's book entry, "*voyage not completed*". This was a stamp in a seaman's book that denoted the seaman had either jumped ship or had been discharged for some other reason. This amounted to a bad mark that reflected badly on anyone pursuing a seagoing career. What stood in my favour was the fact that I had re-joined the vessel in Sydney and completed the voyage without incident. This gave rise to a second stamp of "*VG*" very good. This supplied me with ammunition for my forthcoming tribunal with the shipping federation. I loved the sea life and it was my intention to fight hard to keep my position in the Merchant Navy.

The airport was a short distance from the port and built on a peninsula, which extended into the bay. I flew back to the UK by British United Airways aka BUA. As the plane taxied and lifted into the skies, we witnessed spectacular panoramic views of the harbour and mountain range. As our aircraft slowly circled over the bay, I glanced down at the Cape Wrath belching black smoke into the clear Mediterranean air. I felt no sadness, only relief and excitement; I was on my way home.

The journey home was longer than expected; we had to fly into Stanstead airport, then catch a train into Euston station, before boarding another train to Liverpool.

The train pulled into Lime Street Station, Liverpool my hometown! A warm feeling of nostalgia washed over me as I reacquainted myself with my surroundings. It's strange how your hometown can generate such feelings.

Late afternoon the taxi drew up outside my home, I was surprised to find a huge homemade welcome home banner greeting me. Before I could pay the taxi driver, my family and Bob and Eileen came to the door. Mum gave me a big hug and said, "*I thought I'd never see you again*". It was such a wonderful feeling to be home with friends and family, we had so much to talk about.

A party had been arranged and throughout the day friends and relations turned up at the house. By 8pm the house was bursting at the seams. Dad had served up a Chinese banquet. We sat as I recounted some of the things I'd been up to. This went on until the early hours of the morning. I was devastated to find that during my absence our dog Trixie had died. Trixie was part of the family, for weeks I had had thoughts of walking Trixie through the woods and down to Oglet shore once again. Alas, it was not to be. Mum told me that Trixie would sit waiting at the door for my return.

Prior to my tribunal, quite a few members of the crew had lodged complaints. The ship also had a high incidence of desertion, including one junior officer. This helped supply me with ammunition for my defence. I was let off with a caution and then allowed to continue my seagoing career.

I am sure the fact that I had re-joined the ship in Sydney and for that part of the voyage was awarded two VGs in my discharge book, helped to influence the committee.

I was offered a position on the "*Empress of Canada*" as trainee chef. I started my training on the sauce corner and was told, my tuition would progress through the various departments. However this came to a sudden end with the seaman's strike on May 16 1966. We heard about it halfway across the Atlantic on our way to St John Newfoundland. The crew agreed to complete the trip taking in Quebec and then returning to Liverpool before any action was taken. The majority of the crew secretly hoped the strike would be over by then. I was devastated; The Empress of Canada was a beautiful ship that offered me training, to progress in my career. Unfortunately, the strike continued for another six weeks, so my time on passenger ships was prematurely curtailed.

The Empress of Canada

As a footnote I leave you with one more story, it is about my first trip after the seaman's strike. Although I can recount many more tales, at present I have no plans to write another book.

I feel obliged to add this story, because of the help in rekindling lost memories I received from Knud (Ken) Rasmussen. We sailed together on a ship called Lucigen.

Luck of the draw

Three weeks after the strike ended, I was still trying to find a ship. The strike had created a glut of seamen on the pool, providing many opportunities for foreign seamen to step into British positions. Daily I would turn up at the shipping office situated on Mann Island. There would always be a long queue of other seaman, no matter how early I managed to arrive. Jobs were in short supply, as men scrambled for the opportunity to secure positions. The feeling was that dealings were not entirely above board. One chap, who was ahead in the queue, placed a ten-shilling note in his book. He was then sent through to the next office, and allegedly directed to a choice of vessels. It seemed so blatant that a huge row erupted; scuffles broke out and angry voices grew louder. The shipping pool, fearing a riot called the police. Police in numbers arrived and ejected the so-called troublemakers. Most of the men had been out of work for approximately six to ten weeks; they had families to support and to see such goings on created mistrust and acrimony. Again, they informed me that there were no jobs available, but to call back in a few days. This was becoming a habit and I began to wonder if this was another way to inform me that my days at sea were over.

Dejected, I boarded the 82D bus at the Pier Head and made my way home, with thoughts of phoning different shipping lines, not the done thing but money was running out, it was no fun being home short of cash. When I arrived home mum met me at the door carrying a telegram. "*It's the Shipping Federation*" she said, "*They want you to fly out to Tenerife tomorrow morning to join a ship on its way to India*". I was to join a tanker called the Lucigen, which was owned by Moss Tankers, part of the Cunard Group. She had a gross tonnage of 12324.

MV Lucigen

India seemed an exotic colourful place, it offered a fascinating new culture to absorb and take in. I wasted no time in accepting and getting my things ready to go. My Sister Davina organised the washing and ironing. As the eldest, she was a mother hen; helping with the running of the Ng household and looking after everyone. This trait has followed throughout her life, always putting others first, one of life's carers. After getting my case packed I organised a flight to Tenerife.

After all the rush I arrived in Santa Cruz, Tenerife two days early, seemingly the ship had engine trouble and had to limp into port to effect repairs. The port agents had to put me up in a hotel, so I was able to spend some time as a tourist, but as I didn't have enough money on me, it was all mainly down to walking and taking in the sights. As I boarded the ship, a strong smell of oil greeted me, I wondered if this was what I would have to live with for the next three months or so. I was glad to discover that the smell of oil was due to the ship bunkering, taking on fuel for the trip ahead. Within hours, the air had cleared and a fresh sea breeze cleared all traces as we navigated out into the Atlantic Ocean.

The chief cook was a big man named Ken Rasmussen born in Denmark but married and resident in Liverpool. A great guy who I have kept in touch with to this day, indeed we still procrastinate over our seagoing days. Ken told me later that he had watched me boarding and had mistaken me as Jewish. Throughout my life I have been taken as Italian, Spanish, Portuguese, but hardly ever as Chinese origin, so Jewish was a new one for me; I must have a cosmopolitan look.

It was quite a well-ordered galley and I was happy to find a dough-mixing machine, a first for me as in the past we had to knead all the dough by hand, bent over a large tub. Not very hygienic as in hot climates there was practically no need to add salt to the mix, one's own sweat took care of that! So, making the dough in small batches instead of one big one and then combining it all together, was much easier and took all the hard work out of the equation, leaving me more time to concentrate on the pastry side.

We left the Canary Islands and set sail for the Suez Canal to gain entrance to the Indian Ocean and on towards our destination Kandla, which sits in the Bay of Kutch and lies on the Indian Pakistani Border. Our journey, curtailed with more engine trouble, meant that the ship could only limp into the port of Malta. The bustling port was full; no berths available, so we had to anchor and tie up to one of the pontoons mid harbour. Only 250 yards from the quayside Ken and I decided to swim ashore to taste the delights of a cool beer from one of the quayside bars. I was still not a strong swimmer, but I was quite happy to attempt the 250 yards or so. We pulled ourselves out of the cool waters into the hot sunshine and had dried out in minutes. We then spent two relaxing hours sipping beer and watching the daily activities all around us. We watched the aircraft carrier "*Ark Royal*" entering the port; her sailors resplendent in uniform lined the deck as if in salute; the aircraft, wings up, formed a great backdrop. A party of excited schoolchildren lined the harbour, in white and red uniform; they cheered waving small Union flags. Labourers stopped work and gazed in awe, bar staff halted what they were doing. The whole occasion made me proud to be British. The carrier dwarfed our vessel as she took position on the next pontoon, in the distance I could hear a brass band play.

All too soon it was time to make our way back to work and prepare the evening meal. Sunshine and beer took over our bodies as we bravely dived into the harbour and struck out back to reality. After a hundred yards or so, I noticed toilet paper in the water. I scanned around to find I was swimming in a sea of sewage; floaters of all sizes surrounded me. Ken being a stronger swimmer was already climbing the gangway. Panicking and holding your breath just does not go together. I felt cramp seize one of my legs and I was struggling to stay afloat when the next cramp took my other leg. I felt myself go under, come up gasp for air then go under again. I remember thinking, this is what it must be like to die, as between mouthfuls of sewage and air I yelled for help. Coughing and spluttering, I felt myself being dragged into a small boat. Thankfully, one of the small harbour boats had witnessed my difficulty and came to my rescue. It seems the Ark Royal had emptied some sewage into the harbour; an act that would not be allowed today, even in the sixties, I think such an act would have been frowned upon.

I spent the next hour in the shower and gargling, I was the butt of cruel jokes for the next week, as everybody thought it was funny except me. However, the next laugh was on Ken. A couple of months earlier, he had bought a so-called electric blue silk shirt in India, it was his pride and joy. The next time we didn't swim ashore again but instead, waited for the hourly boat. After a few minutes the boat headed nose first into the quayside, I stood up picked up the rope to tie up, Ken grabbed the rope from me and said, "*I'll do that*". He stepped from the boat, missed the quay in his haste and with a huge splash fell into the harbour. I reached to pull him out. He was soaking wet and looked such a sight. The shirt had shrunk a good ten inches exposing his midriff, buttons straining on the cotton. Everyone in the boat fell about laughing, so it was shirt off and into town to buy a new tee shirt. The crew now had another target for their cruel jokes; at least it gave me some respite.

It must have been 30th July 1966 as we were listening to the World Cup final on the BBC World Service. We were halfway through the Suez Canal and experiencing some trouble with the radio reception. Then we heard those immortal words from commentator Ken Wolstenholme. "*And here comes Hurst...some people are on the pitch, they think it's all over, it is now! It's four!*" We all celebrated wildly except for some Scottish members of the crew, who argued that the Germans were the far better team, although it was just harmless banter; which is played out by football fans worldwide.

Our destination Kandla in the Gulf of Kutch was a new port created in 1963 after the loss of Karachi to Pakistan. It was a port built to accept cargo for northern India, indeed today is now one of the largest cargo handling ports in India. Back in 1966 it was still in its infancy, poverty was rife most of people lived in abject poverty in shantytowns awash with raw sewage and human desolation.

I never knew what poverty was until that day in 1966 when two dogs woke my senses to it. We pulled alongside just after lunch and I was carving a leg of lamb for cold meats that night. I noticed two scrawny dogs rooting around the pier; they looked as though they had not been fed in ages. I took pity and threw them the bone. Before the bone hit the wharf two men were fighting over it, the poor dogs didn't get a chance. I realised then that I had just witnessed life on the edge. It put a completely new perspective on life, only for the luck of the draw, our lives could be very different, never since then have I felt badly off.

Still euphoric about our World Cup win, we formed our ship's own team. White shorts, tee shirts and sports socks became our football kit. The ship's agent arranged a match with the locals. We set up a football pitch on a large piece of barren land just outside the dock gates with ample room for a large crowd of locals from outlying villages to watch.

What idiots we must have looked as we went out onto the pitch all dressed immaculately while the locals played in what they were wearing, that meant in all manner of colours and some barefoot. I was embarrassed and felt like crawling back to the ship to hide. The pitch was a rock-strewn piece of land baked hard by the unrelenting sun, very different from the grassy pitches back home. This was going to be difficult as even in bare feet the locals played as if they had steel-capped working boots on. We were going down like flies indeed. I came off and was substituted after stubbing my big toe on a rock. I limped off in absolute agony. Before I reached the side-lines, my toe had doubled in size and I had trouble removing my boot.

The game carried on amongst frequent whistle blowing by the captain who had been appointed referee, the game would stop and he would count how many of the locals had jumped from the crowd to join in; all heavily disguised by the mish-mash of clothing they wore. At one juncture, they had sixteen players on the pitch. It was turning into a comedy and at times felt like we were all participants in a carry on film. Eventually, the game settled down and we were leading 2-1 when all hell broke loose. A large ambling cow pushed its way through the crowd and onto the pitch. We tried to usher it off but it just would not move and stood defiantly in the goalmouth, one of the sailors against better judgement kicked it up the backside. What was he thinking? Cows are sacred in India. The pitch was invaded by all and sundry, making a beeline for the guilty one. We formed a protective barrier and had to fight and shove our way back to the safety of the gangway. Unfortunately, the game was abandoned and the inconsiderate sailor had to refrain from going ashore again in that port.

The next day the port agent drove me in the agents battered army type jeep to a field hospital about 40 miles away to have my foot tended to, which had become steadily worse. We bounced around the vehicle, through shantytowns amid the desolation. Every time the vehicle came to a halt, children appeared with hands outstretched, begging. The only thing I had to offer was my lunch box. It would not hurt me to go hungry for a day. Hands reached out, from the imploring smiling faces of barefoot children in rags; each little voice trying to shout louder than the next, drawing attention to their individual needs. My lunch box evaporated into the crowd before I had time to distribute the contents. As we were only ten minutes from the ship, I asked the driver if we could go back to the ship and get some more food to give away. He replied, "*No matter how much food you bring you will need more, we will never get to the doctor, you must close your eyes. This is India and you alone can't change things*". I had also prepared a lunch box for the agent, but that stayed hidden under his seat. Those smiling hungry pleading faces will forever paint a picture in my thoughts.

As I hobbled up to what was just a large tent on the edge of a sprawling small town, I noticed a very long winding queue, filled with women, children and old people, who were patiently waiting to see the medical team. The midday sun was beating down, beads of sweat formed rivulets down the weary faces. I was horrified when I was whisked to the front of the queue, past people obviously more sick than I was. I protested and said, "*I would rather forgo any treatment than jump the queue*". The Indian agent cast aside my protests. He roughly pushed me ahead.

I had a small fracture. The medic tended to it and I left in more pain than I had arrived with. I was struck by the unfairness of society and felt morally wrong that I had played a part in it.

Corruption was rife. Berthed next to us was an American freighter unloading sacks of rice, all stamped with "*A present from the people of the US*". As we walked around the back of the sheds, we noticed that the sacks were being interfered with before being loaded onto trucks. The stamp now read "*A present from the people of the USSR*". One of our officers reported it to the captain of the American ship. They stopped unloading the ship until they could tighten security and another stamp was added to show in brackets (United States). In that time of cold war, I suppose it was a cheap way for the communists to curry favour.

Leaving India made me reflect on life and realise what a privileged world I live in. Luck of the draw governs our very existence and I count myself lucky to be born and raised in a country with very few real hardships. It is down to the individual, to make the most of what they have been gifted with. I shall forever have instilled in my mind-set, that if ever I feel down or hard done to, I cast my thoughts back to the people fighting off dogs to eat leftover scraps.

Life has been good to me.

Epilogue

I enjoyed my seagoing days, although at times things were difficult, the good times always come to the fore. The Merchant Navy gave me as a young man a wide perspective of the world and the way people lived in far away places. I feel privileged to have experienced many different cultures and attitudes across the world and very fortunate to have benefited in the lessons of life that the Merchant Navy taught me.

I still travel the world, but now with my wife as passengers on cruise ships. Although not as action packed as my navy days, it never ceases to amaze me how the world has changed, sometimes for better and sometimes for the worse. The country that made the most impression on me was and will always be New Zealand. One day I hope to return and pay a visit, I am getting to the age that it's becoming a diminishing dream, but throughout my life there have been many twists and turns, so who knows what the future holds.

I have revisited some so-called third world countries and seen that they have completely turned around and are now shining lights in prosperity, while others have languished in the doldrums.

The passage of time has taken a toll and I have done my best to keep things in the correct time frame. Please take into account that there will be anomalies, on dates and order of events.

For the rest of my life, I am sure that many ex mariners will agree and say the same -

The sea will be 'Always In My Blood'.

Mum and dad in 1986

*March 2015 from left: Lynne, Gar, Barbara, Robert and
Sandi - In front: Jenny and Dee*

Acknowledgments

To my wife Jade, who has stood by me through thick and thin, on reflection, I wonder how she puts up with me.

To both my sons Michael and Kevin, who have made me very proud with their achievements in life; for them it is just the early stages; I look forward to even greater things.

To Claire and Melanie my daughters in law, I thank them for the enrichment they have brought to our close-knit family.

To our wonderful grandchildren, Anna Faye and Cameron who light up my heart each time I see them. A special mention must go to Victoria and Daniel, who are grandchildren in all but name. I leave a space for any future grandchildren

To my brother Gar, sisters Davina, Lynne, Jennifer, Sandi, Barbara and Dolly Sue - the amazing thing is we have never fallen out with each other. This is simply due to the close family bond we inherited from our wonderful parents, May and Hung.

To close and distant relatives even with our busy lives we should get together more often. It is so sad to lose contact.

I could not write this dedication without mentioning Bob and Eileen Roberts who we have all known since childhood, such is our love for them; they are almost flesh and blood.

I am fortunate to have met many good people through the years, both in work and play, far too many to mention, but all who I know on first name terms are included.

My thanks go to my sisters Lynne and Sandi for correcting my many grammar and punctuation errors. I was never a great scholar, the book just staggered and tumbled from my distant memories. Thank you all for your tireless energy and patience.

My friend Will Howell also deserves a mention for the support and encouragement and for keeping my computer firing on all cylinders.

Finally yet importantly, a special mention must go to Wayne Yeates. Without his friendship and encouragement, I may never have joined the Merchant Navy and I could not have written this book.

Appendix

List of Ships

The following is a list of some of the ships and their respective companies I have sailed and worked on:

Crinan	Denholmes
Barrister	T J Harrison
Author	T J Harrison
Diplomat	T J Harrison
Arcadian	Ellerman & Papayani
Grecian	Ellerman & Papayani
Lancastrian	Ellerman & Papayani
Florian	Ellerman & Papayani
MV Pearl	Gem Line
Salinas	PSNC
Sarmiento	PSNC
Cape Wrath	Lyle Shipping Company
Tewksbury	Houlder Brothers
Westbury	Houlder Brothers
Shaftesbury	Houlder Brothers
Queensbury	Houlder Brothers
Oswestry Grange	Houlder Brothers
Empress of Canada	Canadian Pacific
Roland	Lamport and Holt
Dryden	Lamport and Holt
Ronsard	Lamport and Holt
Romney	Lamport and Holt
Amoria	Shell Tankers
Lucigen	Moss Tankers

Liverpool Dockers Nicknames

The Lazy Lawyer -*always sitting on a case*

Diesel Fitter - *he would rummage through the cargo for anything he could steal, was known to exclaim Diesel fitter (These will fit her)*

The Good Sheppard - *walked off a ship with a leg of lamb under his coat*

The Immortal Sergeant - *wore an old Army overcoat with a bullet hole in the back.*

Anything Will Do - *nickname given to a Docker's apprentice who was sent to buy 10 Woodbines (for those of you too young to remember Woodbines, they were budget cigarettes). He asked, "What if they don't have Woodbines?" The reply, "anything will do" He brought back a pork pie!*

Al Capone - *his favourite saying, "where's the gang?*

The Baldy Rabbit - *lend's a tenner I've lost my fare*

Batman - *he won't leave the ship without Robin*

Cinderella - *I've got to be away by twelve*

The London Fog - *never lifts*

The Man In Black - *always going to a funeral*

The Piano - *because everyone played on him*

The Reluctant Plumber - *won't do a Tap*

The Clever Fish - *used a long pole to catch the hook as it came down the hold*

The Virgin - *I've never done this before*

The Destroyer - *always looking for a sub*

The Ghost - *always moaning*

The Mirror - *always saying, "What you do reflects on me*

Swan Vestas - *always on strike*

The Coronation Kid - *"she'll crown me when I get home"*

The Spaceman - *always went to Ma's for dinner*

The Cat - *going to Me-Owl girls tonight.*

Notes

Notes

Printed in Great
Britain
by Amazon